Pentecostal Movement and Charismatisation

Approaches – Suggestions – Perspectives

Pentecostal Movement and Charismatisation

Approaches – Suggestions – Perspectives

**A Study Document by the
Advisory Commission for Worldwide Ecumenism
of the Evangelische Kirche in Deutschland
(EKD – Protestant Church in Germany)**

Translation: Neville Williamson

Bibliographische Information der Deutschen Nationalbibliothek
Die Deutsche Nationalbibliothek verzeichnet diese Publikation in der
Deutschen Nationalbibliographie; detaillierte bibliographische Daten
sind im Internet über *http://dnb.dnb.de* abrufbar.

© 2022 by Evangelische Verlagsanstalt GmbH · Leipzig
Printed in Germany

Cover: Anja Haß, Leipzig
Coverabbildung: © Free-Photos/pixabay
Satz: druckhaus köthen GmbH & Co. KG
Druck und Binden: CPI books GmbH, Leck

ISBN 978-3-374-07095-4 // eISBN (PDF) 978-3-374-07096-1

www.eva-leipzig.de

Preliminary Remarks

On a global level, Christianity is growing. However, this cannot be put down mainly to the traditional, post-Reformation churches, but rather to a new, strong branch on the denominational tree: Pentecostal and charismatic churches are experiencing a strong increase in numbers and already comprise a quarter of Christianity worldwide.

The change is particularly momentous in many countries of the Global South. But charismatically orientated groups are also increasingly attractive in Europe. It is particularly young people who appreciate their lively forms of worship. International congregations with a Pentecostal profile live in our midst and in some places they are using Protestant churches and church halls.

This development challenges us to take a closer look, for most of us hardly know what Pentecostal churches are about. Old prejudices and new headlines distort our perception.

For this reason the Council of the Evangelische Kirche in Deutschland (EKD – Protestant Church in Germany) requested its Advisory Commission for Worldwide Ecumenism to prepare a description of this global movement – a kind of travel guide for an unknown terrain. To this end, the commission got into contact with numerous experts who contributed perspectives on the Pentecostal movement from the inside and the outside. There was much to be explored and understood, so that this guide now offers comprehensive orientation.

First of all, here is the most important insight: Pentecostal Christianity is not a clearly definable new "denomination", but a broad movement including highly diverse and also contradictory manifestations. That is why this study document contains numerous "case studies" intended to give an impression of the way in which Pentecostal Christianity manifests itself in different contexts, all over the world as well as in our own country. It makes fascinating reading.

In addition to this differentiated perception, the study document also focuses on theological debate. It identifies a variety of topics with which our theology has been concerned in recent years – for example the rediscovery of the Holy Spirit, or the question of a holistic understanding of creation – and which allow us to enter into a new dialogue with Pentecostal theology. Other typically "Pentecostal" topics offer us theological challenges, such as the question of the reality of evil or the concrete experience of salvation. This document reaches the basic conclusion that both sides can learn a great deal from one another.

At the same time, it does not ignore the fact that it is necessary to reject and clearly contradict certain forms of Pentecostal theology. The partner churches of the EKD in the Global South would not be the last to tell us a thing or two about questionable developments in Pentecostal Christianity, and their voices are heard in this document. It is a question of defining criteria for discerning and distinguishing the spirits – in order to find practical consequences for ecumenism and development cooperation, for example.

This study document is deliberately intended to serve as a starting point, an impetus to take a fresh look at the Pentecostal movement, to take it seriously and to search actively for opportunities to meet it. To this end, it not only provides the necessary background information, but also a host of ideas intended to bring our church into dialogue at various levels.

The Council of the EKD is most grateful to the members of the Advisory Commission for Worldwide Ecumenism, to its chairperson Prof. Dr. Ulrike Link-Wieczorek and the head of the Working Group on Pentecostal Churches, Prof. Dr. Claudia Jahnel, for all they have done. It also thanks the people in many countries with whom the Commission had contact and whose expertise made it possible to present such a comprehensive picture.

The Council hopes that this study document will arouse the curiosity of many people in our church. Those who read it will be well prepared for an ecumenical conversation for which the time is now ripe.

Hanover, September 2021

Bishop Dr Heinrich Bedford-Strohm
Chair of the EKD-Council

Contents

1.	**Introduction: Themes, challenges and goals of the study document**	13
1.1	Growing pluralisation of Christianity	13
1.2	Pentecostal churches and charismatic movements	17
1.3	Challenges for EKD member churches and their theological traditions	18
1.4	Aims, approaches and structure of the study document	21
2.	**The global phenomenon of Pentecostalism**	25
2.1	The beginnings of the Pentecostal movement worldwide and in Germany	25
2.2	Not all Pentecostal churches are the same	35
2.3	Structures and organisational forms in the Pentecostal movement	39
2.4	Dialogues and ecumenical relations	47
	2.4.1 Pentecostalism and the WCC	48
	2.4.2 Further ecumenical relations between the Pentecostal movement and other Christian churches	52
3.	**Theological challenges**	56
3.1	Approaches: The Spirit at the centre	56
3.2	What happens to us: The significance of experience	66
3.3	What guides us: The understanding of scripture	72
3.4	What is all around us: God's work in creation	77
3.5	When we devote ourselves: Christ as Lord and Saviour	82
3.6	What is in store for us: Eschatology and apocalypticism.	87
3.7	What threatens us: Spirits and demons	92
3.8	How we experience salvation: Prayer, healing, blessing, empowerment	98
3.9	What makes us sing: Music and spirituality	115
3.10	How we lead: Charisms, authority and leadership	122
3.11	Where we are sent: Mission and witness.	130

| 3.12 | What unites us: Pentecostal churches and ecumenism | 142 |
| 3.13 | Concluding remarks .... | 157 |

4.	**Religion – Politics – World Responsibility**.........	158
4.1	Approaches	158
4.2	Paradigm shift: From escaping the world to social ethics	161
4.3	Exercising political responsibility	168
4.4	A political theology script: Dominion theology	169
4.5	Aspects of ritual practice in dominion theology	175
4.6	International networks and questions of political ethics in an ecumenical context	183
4.7	World responsibility: Criteria for an ecumenical learning dialogue	188
4.8	State intervention, taking the example of South Africa	194
4.9	Political abuse of religion: Ecumenical dissociation ...	197
4.10	Considerations for gaining competence in development and sustainability	198

5.	**Practical recommendations for ecumenical relations with Pentecostal churches and the charismatic movement**......................................	201
5.1	Initial criteria for the ecumenical journey	201
5.2	Getting to know and understanding each other – at the local level	204
5.3	Institutionalising ecumenical dialogues – the level of the church's governing bodies	213
5.4	Joint world responsibility – Global ecumenism and project work.......................................	216
5.5	Strengthening academic hospitality – Ecumenism with Pentecostals in theology and theological education ...	226

| **6.** | **Summary**...................................... | 229 |

Glossary..	233
Bibliography	255
EKD Advisory Commission for Worldwide Ecumenism and further contributors	261

Case studies: Overview ⊙

Church of God in Germany	28
Church Growth Movement	34
Association of Pentecostal Churches (BFP)	40
Erzhausen Theological Seminary	45
Assemblies of God	57
Living Faith Ministry, Bremen	99
Yoido Full Gospel Church	113
Hillsong	119
Pentecostal Korean congregations in Germany	137
Transnational Chinese True Jesus Church	146
Church of Pentecost, Ghana	153
Charismatisation in Argentina	162
Pentecostalism in Ethiopia	165
Universal Church of the Kingdom of God (Igreja Universal do Reino de Deus)	172
Evangelical Church of the Lutheran Confession in Brazil	177
"Christ for all Nations" – Missionswerk Reinhard Bonnke	192
Evangelical Lutheran Church of Papua New Guinea	218
Evangelical Lutheran Church in Tanzania	222

1. Introduction: Themes, challenges and goals of the study document

1.1 Growing pluralisation of Christianity

Christianity's role and form are currently changing fundamentally. The picture differs according to the place on Earth where people experience the church. From the perspective of the Global South, Christianity is booming and is in fact the fastest spreading religion in the world. Especially in the big cities, for example in Lagos, Rio de Janeiro or Seoul, Christianity is clearly present in the public view, whether in the form of huge new temples built by the megachurches, or of politicians who base their leadership style on Christianity, or just simply in the person of preachers and evangelists who proclaim the gospel in public on the streets. In these contexts, to be a Christian often means that one belongs to a Pentecostal church or an evangelical or charismatic church. Many megachurches are also extremely active in the media, operate their own video channels and are present on all social media channels as globally networked Christianity. However, there are also a host of smaller Pentecostal churches in the favelas and slums of the big cities, where people have a precarious existence and place their hopes on a better future.

From a European and especially a German point of view, the picture is completely different. On the one hand, here in Germany, the number of church members in the mainstream Protestant and Catholic churches is falling; on the other hand, within European Christianity as a whole, the forms of spirituality and the characteristics of the Christian denominations are also changing. In Germany, alongside the main churches cooperating in the Council of Christian Churches in Germany (ACK), a large number of smaller Christian communities has sprung up in the last 20 years or so, gathering for worship and prayer in private homes, rented rooms or church buildings. In some cases these groups can be spiritual awakenings within a denomination, in others they are new congregations without any specific denominational connection. In the Anglican Church in Great Britain (Church of England), such developments in which people try out new forms of church in unusual settings have come to be known since 2004 as *"fresh expressions of church"*. Since then, new expressions of Christian faith have also emerged in many Catholic and Protestant churches in Germany, for example as living room churches, skater services or dinner churches.[1]

Many new congregations are *charismatic* in their spirituality, i.e. faith is expressed in a free form, trusting in the power of God's Spirit, and is characterised by forms of piety emphasising experience and the body. Such charismatic congregations often have a weak institutional foundation and usually operate on an interdenominational basis. International congregations, which use different cultural references and various languages when celebrating their worship services, complete the picture of a Christianity in Germany which is increasingly differentiated and plural. The diversity of international congregations ranges from local church planting to megachurches that are often anchored in global church networks. Christian churches and communities in Germany often exist side by side without really knowing about each other.

---

1 https://www.freshexpressions.de.

For many people, the confessional sense of identity has also transformed into a so-called "multiple belonging": younger people in particular sometimes feel at home both in a historical Protestant church and in a charismatic congregation at the same time; they attend the Pentecostal service, for example, but are also active in the Protestant youth group in their local home church.

This study document focuses attention on these changing contexts within Christianity, the so-called "changing landscapes", meaning the growing pluralisation of Christianity worldwide and in Germany. The emphasis lies on the theology of Pentecostal churches and charismatic renewal movements and on their how important they are for our living together ecumenically in Germany.

When comparing Pentecostal churches and the Charismatic movement on the one hand with the historic Protestant churches on the other hand, the *terminology* is not always distinct. Among the Pentecostals, it is possible to distinguish between traditional Pentecostal churches, neo-Pentecostal churches and charismatic churches. This study document demonstrates that not all Pentecostal churches are alike; there are all kinds of different types and expressions of this Spirit-emphasising piety, according to historical developments and cultural surroundings. It is equally impossible to find a common description for all the traditional churches that emerged from the Reformation. This study document refers to them all as **historical Protestant churches** or **traditional confessional churches** – over against the Pentecostal churches that emerged in the 20th century. In the broadest sense, this subsumes the traditional Protestant denominations which see themselves directly or indirectly as Reformation churches, such as Lutherans, Reformed, United, Presbyterians, Mennonites, Baptists and Methodists. In Germany, the term "historical Protestant churches" is usually taken to mean the regional churches belonging to the EKD, together with the traditional Reformation free churches (Baptists, Mennonites and Methodists among others). English speakers often refer to historical Protestant churches as "mainline churches", but this is misleading, because in most English-speaking countries they do not usually represent the majority of Christians.

1.2 Pentecostal churches and charismatic movements

The origins of the Pentecostal movement lie in various parts of the world. The 1906 revival on → "Azusa Street" in Los Angeles was particularly famous and is considered to be the birthplace of the modern Pentecostal movement. The new Christian faith spread rapidly throughout the world and has adopted many different forms in the meantime (see chapter 2 for more details). Pentecostal churches and charismatic congregations tend to differ according to trends rather than in clearly distinct denominations. The historical and theological roots of the Pentecostal movement go back to the North American Holiness movement of the 19th century and went on to be influenced by the revival movements around the turn of the century. In the course of the 20th century, *charismatic renewal movements* took place, producing independent neo-Pentecostal churches on the one hand and charismatic congregations from originally traditional denominations on the other. Thus charismatic awakenings repeatedly occur within the Roman Catholic Church as well as in denominations of the historical Protestant churches. Pentecostal churches and charismatic renewal movements are growing strongly all over the world. At present, about a quarter of the world's Christianity belongs to a Pentecostal church or a charismatic renewal movement. The geographic focus is undoubtedly in the countries of the Global South. The influx of migrants has also led to an increase in the proportion of Pentecostal churches and charismatic congregations in Germany in recent years, and that will continue. Pentecostal churches are particularly popular in large cities and metropolitan areas, accompanied by a high mobility of their members.

In Germany, numerous Pentecostal churches have joined together in the ⊙ Association of Pentecostal Churches in Germany (BFP), which runs its own training institute (⊙ Erzhausen Theological Seminary) and has been recognised as a public corporation since 1974. In addition, a large number of Pentecostal churches and charismatic congregations exist which do not have any institutional or structural ties to the BFP.

1.3 Challenges for EKD member churches and their theological traditions

In recent decades, a process of rapprochement between traditional confessional churches and Pentecostal churches has begun on various levels, accompanied by a change in mutual perception and a reassessment of former stereotypes. This was urgently necessary, since Pentecostal churches had been regarded as "sects" for a long time by the historical Protestant churches. "Pentecostals" were pejoratively labelled "enthusiastic Christians". From the Pentecostal side, Protestant national churches were described as institutionalised and "dead" Christianity, in which the Holy Spirit was no longer present.

It is good that these mutual negative attributions belong to the past. However, the painful experiences endured by Pentecostal Christians in particular in a range of different contexts have often not yet healed and need to be acknowledged.

The path of rapprochement is strenuous, and at the same time it reveals the widespread *stereotypes and fears* about one another which have developed in both Pentecostal and historical Protestant churches: in historical Protestant churches it is usual to sing traditional hymns with organ accompaniment, in the Pentecostal churches the congregation and their band worship with contemporary Christian praise and worship songs. Protestant churches use formulated prayers written in advance, but Pentecostal churches emphasise free prayer and speaking in tongues (→ glossolalia). The accusation often raised by Pentecostal churches is that the members of traditional churches are not real believers and do not adequately and visibly incorporate fellowship with Jesus Christ and the working of the Holy Spirit into their own lives. In the other direction, traditional confessional churches criticise the Pentecostal churches for instrumentalising the power of the Spirit of God for certain purposes. There are also disputes about the Bible as the centre of faith: the traditional churches are criticised for reading the Bible too much as a historical book (criticism of historical-critical exegesis), while the Pentecostal churches are criticised for understanding the Bible too literally (biblicism). Further grounds for fears and uncertainties in dealing with Pentecostal churches are to be found in historical Protestant churches when it comes to spiritual or faith healing, to practices of casting out demons (→ exorcism) or to the suspicion that neo-Pentecostal churches are only interested in marketing the Christian faith financially. Conversely, believers from Pentecostal congregations sometimes question whether regional church or free church congregations still celebrate their belief in a lively way in their worship services, and how the Holy Spirit is effective in their theology.

Currently, we are in a process in which the diversity of Christianities is clearly emerging worldwide. This makes it necessary for the historical Protestant churches and the Pentecostal churches to be more aware of each other and to come together more strongly than before. It is obvious that they are aware of their common Protestant roots, but find differing forms of expression for their faith. In Germany, there is an official dialogue between the Pentecostal churches and the Protestant Church in Germany, which mainly takes place within the framework of the annual talks between the EKD and the Association of Protestant Free Churches (VEF), to which representatives from Pentecostal churches also belong. At the international level, Pentecostal churches have been members of the World Council of Churches (WCC) since 1961. However, it was only after a decision by the Harare Assembly in 1998 that a Joint Consultative Group was established between the WCC and Pentecostal churches; the first meeting took place in 2000. This WCC consultative group also deals explicitly with controversial theological issues.

Pentecostal churches present challenges to the historical Protestant churches and their theology in ethical, theological, and in some cases political fields. These arise primarily in the cooperation between EKD member churches and their partner churches in the Global South, but also in Germany in connection with contacts to international congregations with a Pentecostal or charismatic profile. The main points of controversy concern lifestyle and sexual orientation, but they can also flare up around the question of the extent to which the Christian faith is instrumentalised for political goals. A major challenge for historical Protestant Christians is the commercialisation of religion in some parts of Pentecostal Christianity. According to the understanding of the so-called prosperity gospel, a person's standing with God is dependent on their personal and economic success. Further critical questions arise with regard to the attitude towards spiritual authority and the danger of spiritual abuse of power (cf. below chap. 3.10).

The dialogue between Pentecostal and historical Protestant churches is therefore crucial for the perception of the respective faith practice, for mutual theological understanding, but also for the distinction and dissociation from each other that is necessary in some areas.

1.4 Aims, approaches and structure of the study document

The present text serves as an orientation within the Evangelische Kirche in Deutschland (EKD – Protestant Church in Germany). In this way, it follows the guiding principle of the Charta Oecumenica (2001), in which the churches committed themselves to "overcome the feeling of self-sufficiency within each church, and to eliminate prejudices; to seek mutual encounters and to be available to help one another".[2]

The study document is addressed to those responsible at the various levels of the EKD, its member churches and agencies, in partner churches and institutions worldwide, including especially those who are active in theological education and in ecumenical institutions.

It aims to encourage member churches of the EKD to encounter Pentecostal churches and charismatic congregations as part of the one Church of Jesus Christ. The guiding criterion of the study document is to promote the ability to speak about the Pentecostal movement and charismatic currents in the diversity of Christianity. Following this ecumenical hermeneutic, the

---

2 Charta Oecumenica. Guidelines for the Growing Cooperation among the Churches in Europe (2001), Chapter II.3: "Moving towards one another".

study document does not confront Pentecostal churches and charismatic movements in a phenomenologically descriptive, distanced, judgmental or apologetic way, but forms an ecumenically open, but also positioned contribution to dialogue. The aim of the study document is to counteract uncertainties on the basis of information and to break down existing stereotypes on the basis of theological orientation. The encounter with the theology and spirituality of Pentecostalism can be helpful in rethinking one's own theological positions in order to gain new insights into one's own theology and faith practice.

Chapter 2 introduces the global phenomenon of Pentecostalism. Beginning with a brief historical overview of Pentecostalism, the chapter provides an overview of the typology of Pentecostal churches and outlines existing ecumenical relationships.

Chapter 3 then unfolds fundamental theological questions that arise in the dialogue with the Pentecostal churches and identifies commonalities, differences and current theological incompatibilities from a systematic-theological perspective.

Chapter 4 looks at the social and political practices of Pentecostal churches and the charismatic movement in social engagement, whereby dissonance and criticism are named and justified.

Chapter 5 formulates practical recommendations for the ecumenical journey with the Pentecostal churches and the charismatic movement, which can be used to shape dialogue and ecumenical cooperation at the various levels of church activity.

Some central terms of the document are explained in a separate *glossary*, which is referred to in the text by an arrow, thus →.

The study document is supplemented by a series of *case studies*, which are referred to in the text by this symbol ☉. On the one hand, these summarise essential contents that are important for the theology, spirituality and practice of Pentecostal churches and the charismatic movement. On the other hand, they present examples of the diversity of Pentecostal churches and charismatic movements. Case studies from the Global South represent the challenges faced by international partner churches of the EKD, its member churches and agencies. They are also exemplary – other, even contrasting examples could be found.

A decisive factor in writing this study document was that it already expresses the dialogue between Pentecostal churches and the EKD. In order to counteract "talking about Pentecostal churches", the study document was developed in cooperation with and with the participation of Pentecostal theologians, as well as in discussion with representatives of various institutes for research on religious and ideological issues.

The authors of this study document come from different backgrounds, and their intensive controversial discussions have accompanied and enriched its drafting. The present text endeavours to take account of the diversity of Christianity and to consciously make room for it. The study pleads for an ecumenically open learning attitude in which differences and commonalities between the EKD and Pentecostal churches or charismatic trends can be identified and churches and congregations mutually encouraged to engage in dialogue.

2. The global phenomenon of Pentecostalism

"Pentecostalism has experienced amazing growth. [...] It is fundamentally an 'ends of the earth', missionary, polycentric, transnational religion. The experience of the Spirit and belief in the world evangelization are hallmarks of Pentecostalism."[3]

The Pentecostal movement is characterised by a unique pace of growth, derived from its strong sense of mission, the direct relation to the Apostolic Age and an eschatological expectation of the coming Kingdom and the redemption of the world. This is how Allan H. Anderson, who can be considered one of the most important researchers of Pentecostalism, characterises the Pentecostal movement. In his book "To the Ends of the Earth" he describes how the Pentecostal movement has decisively changed world Christianity. Following on from this statement of the importance of the Pentecostal movement, this chapter will first trace the way in which the Pentecostal movement emerged and went on to spread throughout the world as well as in the Pentecostal churches and congregations in Germany. This has been a highly differentiated phenomenon from the outset to the present day.

2.1 The beginnings of the Pentecostal movement worldwide and in Germany

At the beginning of the 20th century, Christians in various parts of the world reported that they had had special transcenden-

---

3 *Anderson* 2013, 1 (see bibliography).

tal experiences or had observed them in others, interpreted as the workings of the Holy Spirit. Events in Los Angeles are particularly famous, where on 9 April 1906 believers who were followers of the Afro-American preacher William Seymour experienced special manifestations of the Holy Spirit for the first time. Shortly afterwards, the group, which was joined by growing crowds of men and women of different ethnic backgrounds and social affiliations, moved to a building in 312 Azusa Street. This much-vaunted beginning contains the classic characteristics of Pentecostal identity: a conversion and baptism with the Holy Spirit takes place, at a precise place and time. This experience transcends the boundaries of ethnicity, class and gender. This → "Azusa Street Revival" is considered by many to be the cradle of the Pentecostal movement. But it must be noted that the entire first decade of the new century was permeated by revivals and similar experiences of being blessed with the Holy Spirit, all across the globe. Apart from the spread of Pentecostal testimony in the USA, the most prominent reports came from India, Chile, Norway and Wales. In 1907, a great outpouring of the Spirit (→ "Mukti Revival") occurred in Mukti/India in the state of Maharashtra in the home for widows and orphans founded by Pandita Ramabai. The Methodist Church in Chile was gripped by a spirit of prayer. The descriptions of the outpourings of the Spirit in Valparaiso and Santiago read over long passages like the accounts of the Acts of the Apostles: prophecies, dreams, mocking, healings and speaking in tongues are just some of the phenomena that took place. The revival came to Norway through the Methodist pastor Thomas Ball Barrett. After returning from a trip to the USA, where Barrett himself experienced the outpouring of the Spirit and began to speak in tongues, his sermons triggered a broad revival and spread to neighbouring European countries. Barrett is also designated as the father of the European Pentecostal movement. The German Lutheran pastor Jonathan Paul stayed in Norway until 1907. Since 1890 he had propagated his conversion experience, which moved him theologically into the tradition of the Holiness movement, and after his return from Norway he became an important crystallisation figure of the first wave of the Pentecostal movement in Germany. A revival movement had caught hold of Wales as early as 1904 and also exercised great influence on events in Germany. Thousands of believers in Wales experienced a personal conversion, which they described as a baptism in the Spirit. It was mainly the spiritual leaders of the pietistic Fellowship movement who travelled to Wales from Germany. The first German-speaking historiographer of the Pentecostal movement, Leonhard Steiner, wrote in 1954: "It is almost impossible to determine the year and date of the beginning of the movement. It is also difficult to find a country or a place where it first broke out: spontaneously and almost simultaneously, the Holy Spirit descended on children of God waiting in various parts of the world and filled them."[4]

In Germany, a Whitsun conference which took place in Gnadau in 1888 marks the beginning of the pietistic "Fellowship movement" within the regional Protestant churches. The Pentecostal revivals that took place in Germany from 1905, and especially in 1907, put the Gnadau Association to a severe test. The German Tent Mission, which had been founded in Mülheim an der Ruhr in 1902, held large meetings there around Whitsun in 1905. For weeks, thousands flocked to the tent: "3,000 voices burst out into one song after another. The singing echoes far and wide through the nearby streets, so that the people in the neighbourhood, who usually lounge in the windows and make fun of passers-by, are

---

4   *Steiner* 1954, 18.

⊙ **Case study: Church of God in Germany**

The Protestant free church "Gemeinde Gottes in Deutschland" (Church of God in Germany), which dates back to the work of the German-American Herman Lauster from 1936, is an association of 70 local congregations based on Holy Scripture as the inspired Word of God and the personal confession of Jesus Christ. As part of the international "Church of God" based in Cleveland, Tennessee (USA), it belongs to the worldwide Pentecostal movement. Its theology is based on the five Pentecostal fundamentals of conversion, sanctification, baptism in the Spirit, healing and the expectation of Christ's imminent return. The concern for personal sanctification and social responsibility is of great importance, as is also reflected in a diaconal orientation. The constitution and congregational statutes define the following goals: evangelism, discipleship, church planting, mission, counselling, education, cooperation with other Christians and churches of the same faith.

Starting as a renewal movement in the USA in 1886, the movement has experienced strong growth and now numbers almost 80 million members in 185 countries. Since the turn of the millennium, cooperation with the German Evangelical Alliance (DEA) and the Association of Evangelical Free Churches (VEF) has been intensified.

forced to see and hear that this great movement has taken hold of hundreds and thousands," wrote Ernst Modersohn, at that time a pastor in Mülheim.[5] The events in Mülheim form the background and an important breeding ground for the events that then took

---

5   *Vetter* 2009, 68.

place in 1907, for example in Kassel under the influence of women missionaries from Norway. Another pioneering protagonist, albeit a very ambivalent one, was the evangelist Heinrich Dallmeyer, who travelled with the Norwegian women to the meeting in Kassel. This event, which was planned for one week in July 1907, continued beyond that into August. What happened there – healing, forgiveness and blessings of the spirit, speaking in tongues and states of ecstasy – gained so much attention from the local and national press that the masses of visitors got out of control. On 2 August, the police intervened and broke up the meeting. Reports by representatives of the church were also critical of the events in retrospect: "There were objectionable phenomena such as loud shouting, hissing, prophecies in the name of God. The prophecies took on an increasingly harsh and threatening tone, sins were revealed, anyone who refused was threatened with expulsion."[6] Even well-disposed observers commented on the events in Kassel (then spelt with a C): "God has lit a fire in Cassel, but for the time being it still burns with much smoke and fumes. [...] Let us therefore ask the Lord to cleanse and purify the movement in Cassel from all that is *from below,* so that it may be a blessing for all God's people in Germany."[7] This is the keyword that characterised the following disputes in and with the Gnadauer Verband. Do these experiences come from the endowment with *God's* Spirit or from a spirit *from below*? Heinrich Dallmeyer himself distanced himself from the events in Kassel in the strongest possible terms. He called the power that had taken hold of him and many others there a spirit of lies. This heralded the break between the larger part of the Fellowship movement and the Pentecostal movement. In the → Berlin Declaration

---

6 *Frank Lüdke,* Die Trennung von Pfingstbewegung und Gemeinschaftsbewegung, www.eh-tabor. de/de/die-trennung-von-pfingstbewegung-und-gemeinschaftsbewegung (retrieved 13.5.2020).

7 *Vetter* 2009, 98.

of 15 September 1909, leaders of Protestant regional churches and free churches who came from the Fellowship movement and the Evangelical Alliance stated: "The so-called Pentecostal movement is not from above, but from below; it has many phenomena in common with spiritualism. Demons are at work in it, who, cunningly led by Satan, mingle lies with truth in order to deceive the children of God. In many cases, people ostensibly endowed with the 'gifts of the spirit' have subsequently proved to be possessed. [...] Hateful phenomena, such as falling down, grimacing, trembling, screaming, horrible loud laughter and so on, occur [...] during assemblies. Without determining to what extent this is demonic, hysterical or spiritual, such phenomena are not the work of God."[8] Besides such criticism, the Berlin Declaration, which claims to identify the "lying character of the whole movement", also brings specific arguments of justification theology into play. For example, the Declaration states that it opposes the "unscriptural doctrine of the so-called pure heart". It is not possible to go along with the teaching of the Pentecostal movement that "the 'indwelling sin' is eradicated in a pardoned and sanctified Christian". The authors of the Berlin Declaration see the danger of a "man-made holiness". The German Evangelical Alliance and the → Association of Pentecostal Churches did not overcome this chapter of separation until 1996, when they issued the → Kassel Declaration, stating that the condemnations of 1909 were invalid and formulating a common doctrine of the Holy Spirit. Until 1996 there was no understanding between the pietistic circles in German Protestantism and the Pentecostals. Finally, in 2009, a joint declaration was issued by the Mülheim and Gnadau Associations, bringing the history of separation to a conciliatory conclusion.

---

8   Op. cit. 109.

As early as 1908, the Pentecostal movement formed as a recognisable group, especially under the term "tongues movement". An important meeting place, not yet mentioned here, was Hamburg, where Emil Meyer of the *Strandmission* (a centre for the stranded and homeless) was active. Mülheim remained the centre of the German Pentecostal movement in the following years. This is where the largest Pentecostal meetings were held every year.

The → Mülheim Association was founded in 1913. Until the outbreak of the First World War, there was intensive contact with brothers and sisters in England. After the First World War, free Pentecostal churches outside the Mülheim movement were founded, for example the Elim Churches in Hamburg, Berlin and other cities, which were connected to the tradition of the tent mission. A particularly large congregation developed in Königsberg and other regions and cities in eastern parts of Germany. There was also a Pentecostal influence in the *Deutsche Volksmission entschiedener Christen* and the *Vereinigte Missionsfreunde* in Velbert. These groups were also active in world mission and sent Pentecostal preachers to the Far East.

Opinions differ strongly regarding the role and behaviour of the German Pentecostal movement during the era of National Socialism. Like other free churches, they were faced with the dilemma that they had to come to an arrangement with the National Socialist regime in order to continue their activities, to hold regular worship services and missionary events; otherwise their work would have been by prohibited. Many Elim congregations joined with other free churches to form the Union of Evangelical Free Churches, which was officially recognised by the Nazis in 1942. One may assume that particularly during the war "the German Pentecostal movement accepted the National Socialist view of a Germany that was superior to other nations, which led to arrogance and demarcation [...]"[9] But there is also evidence that some Pentecostal groups and congregations were banned and persecuted during the period of National Socialism.

After the end of the Second World War, different forms of charismatic Christianity can be seen in Germany. While the changes in the western parts of the republic were mainly due to immigration from the former eastern territories of the German Reich, the charismatic congregations in the German Democratic Republic (GDR) developed in a very particular way. In the early 1960s, in a similar way to the charismatisation of many traditional denominational churches worldwide, a movement of congregational renewal started, mostly expressed in prayer, Bible study or fellowship groups. Meetings of this kind were of great importance for the spiritual life of the individual. Essentially, these groups, which were particularly strong in the south (Saxony), remained in the framework of existing Protestant churches without adopting a separate organisational form.[10] In West Germany the different Pentecostal traditions joined together after the Second World War to form the Association of Pentecostal Churches (*Christengemeinden*) in Germany. Many Pentecostals came from the eastern territories and founded new congregations. However, the → Mülheim Association was not prepared to be integrated into a union of Pentecostals in Germany. They did not hold speaking in tongues to be the most important expression of endowment with the Holy Spirit. From the outset, Jonathan Paul had relativised the importance of speaking in tongues

---

9 *Brenner* 2012, 182.
10 Cf. EZW-Orientierungen und Berichte, No. 10.

as a characteristic of the Pentecostal movement, quite in accordance with the position of the Mülheim Association: "We do not hold to the opinion that only those who have come to speak in tongues have received the Holy Spirit. Likewise, speaking in tongues is not in itself proof that someone has been filled with the Holy Spirit. [...] We do not in any way wish to give speaking in tongues a higher value than the Bible does."[11] This position led to the Mülheim Association being accused of foregoing a constitutive feature of the movement.

The most important German-speaking expert on Pentecostalism, Walter Hollenweger, sees Jonathan Paul, thanks to his undogmatic attitude to speaking in tongues, as the founder of an ecumenical orientation of the Pentecostal movement and sums up: "None of the newly formed charismatic communities in Germany has joined the Mülheim movement. It is obvious that ecumenical attitudes and prosaic theological work do not pay off! What counts today is aggressive and market-oriented religion!"[12]

In addition to the development of independent Pentecostal forms of organisation, the charismatic movement in particular has also taken root within the historic Protestant churches. In the 1960s, the "Spiritual Church Renewal in the Protestant Church" *(Geistliche Gemeinde-Erneuerung in der Evangelischen Kirche, GGE)* was founded, focussing, among other things, on the transforming work of the Holy Spirit. There is an equivalent in the Catholic Church with the "Catholic charismatic renewal" movement.

---

11 *Steiner* 1954, 55.
12 *Hollenweger* 1997, 371 f.

⊙ Case study: Church Growth Movement

Although the Church Growth Movement (CGM) is not per se Pentecostal or charismatic, but represents a certain pragmatically oriented paradigm of mission theology – the model of "mission as discipleship" – it is nonetheless partly received and adapted as such in this context. The main concern of the CGM is to make the church grow in numbers on the basis of an understanding of mission emphasising the conversion of individuals. Its programme integrates empirical approaches from sociology, social psychology and marketing. The CGM goes back to the evangelical missiologist Donald McGavran (1897–1990), who first experienced so-called *people's movements* as a missionary in India. He sought to make these fruitful in terms of mission strategy in his book "Understanding Church Growth", which was published in 1970 and in German translation in 1990. His controversial principal thesis is: "People like to become Christians if they do not have to cross barriers of race, class or language to do so" (op. cit., 196, so-called *homogeneous unit principle*). McGavran taught at Fuller Theological Seminary in Pasadena, California, in the School of World Mission and influenced generations of missionaries and pastors. His most important student and successor to the chair of World Mission was C. Peter Wagner (1930–2016), who later incorporated Pentecostal elements into the CGM, especially "spiritual warfare" and healings ("Third Wave"). One of the students at Fuller was the later founder of the Vineyard Church, John Wimber (1934–1997), who also adopted the principles of CGM, connecting them with the practice of healings, signs and wonders (*power evangelism*, cf. Wimber's book "Signs, Wonders, and Church Growth" from 1984).

There is a certain fundamental tension between the empirical methods and pragmatic approach of the CGM and the exceptional work of the Holy Spirit as emphasised in the charismatic and Pentecostal movement.

The evangelical branch of the CGM includes, with various modifications, church development models such as *Willow Creek Community Church* (Bill Hybels) and Rick Warren's *Saddleback Valley Community Church* ("Purpose Driven Church", 1995), which have developed modern, target-group oriented and everyday forms of worship and congregation, but are not themselves charismatic or Pentecostal.

2.2 Not all Pentecostal churches are the same

Today, at least 25 percent of Christians worldwide belong to a congregation in the Pentecostal tradition; in addition, large numbers of Christians in other churches have also developed a charismatic piety and theology. The roughly 615 million Pentecostals throughout the world constitute a range of widely differing traditions. In the bounds of this short description, it is impossible to do justice to all the facets of the later history of Pentecostalism.

It is often said that the Pentecostal movement developed in three waves. This distinction between 1. a classical period of origin, 2. a wave of charismatisation in the established churches and 3. the emergence of Pentecostal megachurches of the neo-Pentecostal variety is considered by some to be inadequat[13]

---

13 *Haustein/Maltese* 2014, 15.

– for example, because it does not properly depict the complex history of the emergence of the "plural and multidirectional network"[14] which is a feature of the Pentecostal movement. Moreover, the phase of the emergence of independent small churches, especially in the countries of the Global South, is not taken into account. The three-wave model was mainly coined by representatives of the neo-Pentecostal movement, who were interested in seeing their own tradition characterised as a new wave and further development of the Pentecostal movement. However, since this classification has become widely accepted despite all the simplifications, it will be followed here and supplemented where necessary.

The first phase is directly related to the **revivals** at the beginning of the 20th century which have been described above (see chapter 2.1). Large churches came into being at this period, such as the ⊙ Assemblies of God, which were founded in the USA in 1914 and represent the main stream of Pentecostals worldwide, the ⊙ Church of God, founded in 1886 in the Baptist tradition, and the International Church of the Foursquare Gospel, founded in 1927 by the evangelist Sister Aimee Semple McPherson. The first phase is marked by the consolidation of the congregations and churches that emerged in the first half of the 20th century. These churches and congregations can be described as the historical Pentecostal churches.

The second phase is often referred to as the **charismatisation** of historical churches. Under the influence of Pentecostal Christians in the vicinity local parishes of the historical churches revised their worship services, their prayer practices and their

---

14 *Brenner* 2012, 171.

community life. Thus, there are now charismatic groups and congregations in all the historical denominational churches (including the Roman Catholic), where the worship traditions are inspired by Pentecostalism. However, they do not limit their influence to the spiritual formation of Christian life, but also have an effect on the way the Bible is interpreted, on opinions regarding moral issues and on theology. The EKD Institute for Research on Religious and Ideological Issues (*Evangelische Zentralstelle für Weltanschauungsfragen – EZW*) dates the beginning of this second phase to the early 1960s.[15]

In a third phase, without any contact to the original Pentecostal churches of the "early days", countless independent churches and congregations emerge, claiming to possess the gifts of the Spirit. It is particularly important to them that they are independent from foreign missionary activities. As already mentioned, the protagonists of this phase are the ones who coined the concept of so-called "waves" in which the Holy Spirit came back into focus, and this third "wave" is often also critically known as **neo-Pentecostalism.** On the one hand, this includes the → megachurches of the late 20th century (for example ⊙ Hillsong, ⊙ Yoido Full Gospel Church and ⊙ Igreja Universal do Reino de Deus), but also the countless small independent congregations that came into being after someone received a calling, a vision or a prophecy in a dream. Sometimes there is talk of a "mushrooming of churches", as these churches suddenly shoot up in many places like mushrooms. In many countries they can be found on every street corner; they hold their services and prayer meetings in private houses, but also in precarious places, for example in garages on plastic chairs, because

---

15 *Hempelmann* 2015, see also www.ezw-berlin.de/html/3_182.php (retrieved 20.4.2021).

many of these smaller Pentecostal churches share the everyday cares and lives of their members. The meetings are loud and spill out into the street. The churches give themselves fanciful names and make extravagant claims: "Church of the One True Word", "Lion of Judah Church", "Top Galactical Evangelical Church", "Church of Jesus Alone". Many, but not all, of these third-wave churches and congregations are professionals in the use of the media and heavily focused on growth. The criticism levelled at this movement is that it commercialises Christianity, because founding a church can be a money-making business which secures someone's livelihood.

It is tempting to imagine that Pentecostalism developed in these three steps and thus make the phenomenon manageable. But this hardly does justice to the real phenomenon. It is difficult to draw a line between the original churches and congregations of people who have turned to Pentecostal/Charismatic piety and the new communities. Many Christians have multiple affiliations, choosing different Christian offers and messages for different life situations and questions. This casts doubt on any statistic that assesses church affiliation on the basis of one hundred percent membership. There are only a very few countries in the world where the membership of denominations and local churches can be so clearly and rigidly defined – and registered – as in Germany. The theological and social, ethical and political orientation of the Pentecostal churches covers the entire spectrum of possible positions. In none of the following questions would all churches of the Pentecostal movement give a common answer:

- ■ Are women admitted to the preaching ministry?
- ■ Is it the task of the church to be involved in social work without missionary interests?

- Are men allowed to have sexual desire and love for men, and women for women?
- Is faith in Jesus Christ necessary for salvation?
- Can the Bible contain errors?
- Should the different churches work together ecumenically?
- Are God's blessings, and the goods he bestows to express them, his way of rewarding believers?
- Should one enter into dialogue about religion and faith with people who belong to another religion without wanting to convince them of one's own faith?
- Is a Christian allowed to smoke or drink alcohol?
- Is it only a person who can speak in tongues that has experienced a baptism in the Holy Spirit?

Such a catalogue of questions also makes it clear that there is a similarity between the very heterogeneous Pentecostal movement and the historical Protestant churches, in that basic convictions constituting hallmarks of identity and solidarity transcend denominational boundaries. Differences concerning these questions can be the cause of splits in churches and congregations, a particular danger in Pentecostal communities which strongly emphasise the individual experience of the Spirit. But there can also be friendships, connections and unions across church boundaries.

2.3 Structures and organisational forms in the Pentecostal movement

In Germany, the Pentecostal movement is largely organised in the ⊙ Association of Pentecostal Churches (*Bund Freikirchlicher Pfingstgemeinden – BFP*). It has about 850 congregations num-

⊙ Case study: Association of Pentecostal Churches (BFP)

The Association of Pentecostal Churches (*Bund Freikirchlicher Pfingstgemeinden – BFP*), which has been in existence for 60 years, is a federation of congregations with more than 830 local churches; as an evangelical Pentecostal free church in Germany, it forms part of the worldwide Pentecostal movement which emerged from the 19th century revival movement. The most important characteristics are the belief in the inspiration of Holy Scripture as the Word of God, the personal relationship to Jesus Christ as Saviour, being born again through the Holy Spirit, baptism in the Spirit, orientation towards the example of the Early Christians by practising the charismatic gifts, eschatological expectation and the commitment to mission. As an evangelical free church, it advocates the separation of church and state. It also advocates freedom of belief, conscience and assembly. This is the basis of fellowship in faith and service with other groups from the Pentecostal and Charismatic movements, the free churches and many local congregations within the Evangelical Alliance. On a local and regional level, the congregations maintain contact with the Council of Christian Churches (ACK). The BFP is a member of the Association of Evangelical Free Churches (VEF). The BFP holds to the principle that the local congregation is independent on the one hand, but committed to the affiliation to this free church federation on the other. The leadership of the BFP is in the hands of the executive board and the presidium. The membership, fellowship and ministries are described in the constitution and guidelines of the BFP.

The activities of the Association include the Action Committee for Persecuted Christians, the Forum Theology and

Congregation, the Theological Seminary in Erzhausen, the church planting work, the federal youth organisation, the initiative Women with Vision and the Federal Association of Social Services for Free Church Pentecostal Congregations. The BFP also strives to integrate migrant congregations. According to BFP statistics, at the beginning of 2019 there were a total of 836 congregations, of which 511 were German congregations (61.1 percent), and 325 were of a different language and origin (38.9 percent), meaning that the proportion of congregations with a migration background has grown disproportionately.

The BFP is a guest member and active participant in the Council of Christian Churches in Germany. The EKD and VEF meet once a year for discussions. In August 2016, the BFP published a report entitled "Baptism in the Association of Pentecostal Churches", presenting 15 theses concerning the understanding and practice of baptism in the BFP as well as the interdenominationally important questions of membership and church unity with regard to baptism. In March 2019, the VEF and the EKD held a joint conference on the topic of baptism, at which the BFP took part. The aim of the discussions was to overcome old perceptions which were discriminatory and disparaging.* The topics discussed also include the question of authorisation for religious education in schools. In addition to the theological discussions, work is going on at the practical level. One example of a bilateral EKD-VEF document is the joint manual for church congregations on dealing with baptismal requests from asylum seekers.**

---

* Cf. the documentation: *Neue Perspektiven auf die Taufe. Begegnung und Erfahrungsaustausch der Vereinigung Evangelischer Freikirchen e.V. (VEF) und der Evangelischen Kirche in Deutschland (EKD)*, Theologische Hochschule Reutlingen, 6/7 March 2019 = epd-Dokumentation 14/2020. Here the 15 theses of the BFP are printed on pp. 41 f.

** https://www.ekd.de/ekd_de/ds_doc/taufbegehren_von_asylsuchenden_2013.pdf

bering roughly 65,000 members nationwide. In recent years, the BFP has grown, because Pentecostal international congregations have joined and now play a self-confident role in Christian life in Germany. One third of the congregations are organised in the Association of International Congregations within the BFP. Since 2011, the BFP has been a guest member of the Council of Christian Churches in Germany (ACK) at the national level. In different parts of the country, the contacts between BFP churches and other Protestants have varied greatly in intensity in the past years.

In Germany as in other countries there are many different kinds of piety and faith that can be attributed to the Pentecostal movement. This is a result, among other things, of the diversity of Pentecostal traditions which are meanwhile to be found in the international congregations in Germany. But there is also a variety of trends within the German Pentecostal congregations, which are often marked by a strong internationality. The spectrum ranges from long-established congregations that now provide nursing homes for their elderly members, pop-up churches that use social media to let people know at short notice where the next church service will be held, to missionary project churches that help in the social shaping of their neighbourhoods. In Germany, the ethical and theological orientation of Pentecostal churches is usually indistinguishable from evangelical positions, so that they sometimes have to put up with the criticism that they are just evangelicals who practise speaking in tongues. The implication of such criticism, however, is that one hopes and expects that Pentecostals, with their experience of the Spirit, might bring a breadth and flexibility to the theology and the life of Christians that is impossible in the mainstream churches or the evangelical free churches.

The ecumenical contact between regional Protestant congregations and their Pentecostal neighbours often comes about due to the relationships with international congregations wanting to rent church buildings and halls. Here the intercultural distance makes it easier to experience and tolerate denominational differences. Thanks to this cultural difference, the two sides meet in a "third space", which relativises the confessional differences. Since one has already entered the mode of a new intercultural perspective, it is sometimes easier to integrate a second new perspective. This may well become a promising opportunity for new encounters between Pentecostal Christians and those from the Protestant churches. The resulting dialogue concerns neighbourliness, hospitality and sharing everyday life, which can open up new horizons and also offer opportunities for theologically qualified exchange of views. To put it simply: by entering into contact with another culture, I already imply my openness towards another form of faith. Mutual understanding for differences in belief comes more naturally and peaceably when people of different cultures meet each other.

The pastors of the BFP congregations in Germany are trained in the ⊙ Erzhausen Theological Seminary, holding very close connections to practical work in congregations. In contrast to other free churches in Germany, it is not customary for candidates for the pastorate in the BFP to go to study at the theological faculties of state universities for a few semesters. However, many of the students at state institutions who are training for the teaching profession feel close to the Pentecostal movement and introduce aspects of Pentecostal piety into the courses.

On a global level, the Pentecostal education system is very complex. In some countries there are large private universities owned by Pentecostal sponsors (e.g. the Pentecostal University College in Accra/Ghana), which have their own faculties for theology and religious studies, but also offer many other academic disciplines at a high level, subsuming them under the common slogan "Empowered to Serve". Elsewhere, Pentecostals make use of the academic theological education offered by the historical denominations, thereby changing the face of their classical institutions (for example, at the Escola Superior de Teologia in São Leopoldo/Brazil, a Lutheran theological college). In most cases, the ministers of the Pentecostal churches are trained in their own seminaries. Some neo-Pentecostal churches consider theological training unreasonable and superfluous. God calls the church leader into his task, and Bible study in private and in groups together with the supervision by a senior pastor is considered adequate as preparation for the leadership of a local church. Academic theology is still seen sceptically in wide circles of the Pentecostal movement. However, many people from Pentecostal congregations in the Global South are relatively unprejudiced concerning theological training at western universities – thus the University of Applied Sciences for Intercultural Theology in Hermannsburg (FIT), which offers a liberal curriculum, enjoys a large number of applications from Pentecostal-charismatic theologians.

One difficulty in the dialogue with Pentecostal Christians is the discrepancy between the independent theological work of Pentecostals at universities such as the Fuller Theological Seminary on the one hand and the positions advocated by church leaders and teachers at seminaries and Bible schools on the other. Independent Pentecostal theologians have meanwhile created their own networks, in which they exchange their theological insights and through which they try to influence the theological orientation of the Pentecostal movement. One example is the Latin American network RELEP (*Red Latinoamericana de Estudios Pentecostales*). But the estrangement that separates the Pentecostal movement from its academic theologians is far from being overcome.

⊙ Case study. Erzhausen Theological Seminary

Since 1951, the ⊙ Association of Pentecostal Churches (*Bund Freikirchlicher Pfingstgemeinden – BFP*) has run a theological training school, which was set up with the help of the ⊙ Assemblies of God and has been located in Erzhausen since 1954. Until some time ago the theological seminary was called "Berea".

The teaching staff currently comprises ten professors (in the subjects Old Testament, New Testament, Historical Theology, Systematic Theology, Practical Theology and Missiology). Guest lecturers contribute further experience from congregational practice. Most of the lecturers are also leaders of BFP churches.

The training and further education courses follow the motto "Inspired by Christ – Qualified by His Word – Committed to His Church" and can be taken on a full-time or (in-service) part-time basis. The prerequisite is a secondary school education with an intermediate or university entrance qualification as well as three years of vocational training. The eight-semester full-time programme (including one practical semester) qualifies students for pastoral or missionary service. The modular study programme (B.A.) is associated with the distance learning system of the American-Pentecostal International Correspondence Institute (ICI Germany). There are also so-called integration courses which give trained church leaders from other denominations access to ministry in a BFP church. A distinction is made here between candidates from other denominations, who have to attend six modules, and pastors from the worldwide Pentecostal movement, who only have to attend three modules.

A total of 230 candidates are currently studying in Erzhausen, 65 of them full-time. Over 40 per cent of the current students have a migration background. This figure shows how much the BFP is appealing to the international congregations in Germany, crossing borders by way of theological education and allowing room for transformation of its own church.

The range of courses offered by the Theological Seminary, which are described in detail on the website, contains all the classical areas of theology. There are just a few courses which would not be included among the courses of traditional denominations, such as a seminar on "Church Planting". The event format "Spiritual Foundations" also indicates the special character of the training at the seminary in contrast to classical theological studies. It covers discipleship, service and leadership as well as angelology and exorcism.

Applicants to the theological seminary are not just expected to submit various documents, but also to give information on the following questions about their spiritual development: "When were you converted? When were you baptised and in which church? What experience do you have with the baptism in the Holy Spirit? Which church do you belong to? Have you worked in any ministry in the church? If yes, in which one? What were you responsible for? If no, why not?" In addition to the coursework, the students are expected to take part in the spiritual life of the seminary at the regular worship services and the monthly day of prayer.

The seminary accepts guest students and also offers a course in "Leadership" which is part of the two-year practical training for the BFP pastors. Credits can be recognized for experience and for studies at other training centres, in particular at those with which Erzhausen has bilateral agreements, such as the Baptist Seminary in Elstal and the European Theological Seminary of the German Church of God in Kniebis near Freudenstadt. Participation in courses of the so-called *Momentum College* (www.momentumcollege.de) can also earn credits for studies at the seminary in Erzhausen. Momentum College is independent of the BFP and offers an evangelical programme, for example in the areas of leadership training, business, film, youth ministry, worship, social work and music production. There is no cooperation with theological faculties at German universities and colleges.

2.4 Dialogues and ecumenical relations

The Norwegian pastor Thomas B. Barratt is famously quoted as saying that Pentecostals are Lutherans in their understanding of salvation, Baptists when it comes to baptism and Methodists for sanctification, Salvationists by their aggressive evangelistic practice, but Pentecostals in their understanding of baptism in the Spirit. Theoretically, this would make them excellently prepared for and interested in ecumenical connections and exchange of views. However, in the wide-ranging and heterogeneous spectrum of Pentecostal and charismatic churches and networks, there are strongly anti-ecumenical convictions, but also interest in and openness for ecumenical dialogue on a local, national and international level.

This chapter first describes the history and status of the Pentecostal movement's relationship with the World Council of Churches. In a second step, the bilateral relations between Pentecostalism and the Orthodox and Roman Catholic Churches as well as with the global communion of Lutheran and Reformed churches are briefly outlined as examples.

2.4.1 Pentecostalism and the WCC

a) Although in the first three decades the great majority of Pentecostal churches were anti-ecumenical, there were also Pentecostals who were open to ecumenical cooperation and dialogue. From the first years after the founding of the Ecumenical Council in 1948, one should make special mention of the US-Americans David J. Du Plessis, Donald Gee and J. Roswell Flower. They kept in touch with the International Missionary Council, which was institutionally independent of the WCC until 1961.

In 1961, the first Pentecostal churches were admitted as official members of the WCC: among them the two Chilean churches "Iglesia Pentecostal de Chile" and the "Missión Iglesia Pentecostal", later the "Igreja Evangélica Pentecostal do Brasil para Cristo" (Manoel de Mello) from Brazil, and then as from 1972 the "International Evangelical Church and Missionary Association". Today, the WCC has seven Pentecostal member churches, together with some of the ⊙ African Instituted Churches (AIC), which are also of a Pentecostal nature (e.g. Church of the Lord Aladura, Nigeria); the Organisation of African Instituted Churches (OAIC) is an associate member of the All African Council of Churches and cooperates closely with the WCC.

b) A matter of controversy between the WCC and Pentecostal churches is the question of how theology is positioned in relationship to politics. In the 1970s, the WCC made various attempts to engage more broadly with the Pentecostal movement. Some Pentecostal churches rejected the WCC as being "anti-Western". When the evangelical Lausanne movement was founded in 1974, it served a number of Pentecostal churches as a way of making international connections with Christians all over the world and beyond the boundaries of their own community. Additionally, or as an alternative, many churches also found a multilateral home in the → Pentecostal World Fellowship or in the respective National Pentecostal Fellowships.

The community that was united in the Lausanne movement avoided the term "ecumenism". "Ecumenism" was seen as the field of the World Council of Churches, in which the liberation theologies of Latin America and other regions of the world had played an important role since the 1960 s and 1970s, and questions such as the legitimacy of revolutions, the justification of resistance and violence, and the relationship between justice and peace were on the agenda.

A special sign of the WCC's outstretched hand and interest in Pentecostalism, which was also perceived as such by Pentecostals, was a letter from the general secretary Philip Potter to all member churches in August 1979 asking "to help him understand the charismatic movement and address the issues that need to be discussed in this context".

c) A number of Pentecostal churches, especially in African countries, which are not affiliated to the WCC as such, are nevertheless members of national and regional councils of churches which are for their part members of the WCC. There they work together with other historical churches, bringing in their particular spiritual and theological character. For example, evangelical, independent and Pentecostal churches belong to each of the 16 national councils of churches currently supported by "Brot für die Welt" (Bread for the World) in Africa and represent on the basis of this ecumenical connection strategic partners of this development organisation.

d) From a very early stage, representatives of the Pentecostal movement were invited to conferences and assemblies of the World Council, for example to the 5th World Missionary Conference in 1952 in Willingen in Germany or to the second WCC Assembly in Evanston in 1954. Representatives of Pentecostal churches were called to serve on the Faith and Order Commission and also to take part in the Commission on World Mission and Evangelism (CWME). The 1982 WCC mission statement "Mission and Evangelism" was integrative and enabled some rapprochements. In 2010, the World Pentecostal Association participated in the conference celebrating the 100th anniversary of the Edinburgh World Mission Conference.

This was preceded by a decisive step for dialogue with the Pentecostal churches: at the Assembly in Canberra in 1991 under the motto "Come, Holy Spirit – Renew the Whole Creation", WCC member churches were urged to recognize congregations of Pentecostal churches "as part of the historical development of the Christian church and its rich diversity", to help foster relationships with Pentecostal churches and to encourage a dialogue between Pentecostals who are open to the ecumenical movement with those churches which are suspicious of ecumenism (see also chapter 4.6). A visible expression of this interest is the permanent "Joint Consultative Group between the WCC and Pentecostals" (JCG), which has been in existence since 2000.

e) A fourth extended circle of connection between the WCC and Pentecostal churches is the → Global Christian Forum, held for the first time at the world level in 2007. The Global Christian Forum, which representatives of the WCC helped to initiate and in which they also have taken on responsibility, is an extended ecumenical platform for dialogue with non-member churches who are nevertheless open to an ecumenical learning journey and exchange with each other. It emerged from an extensive process of discussion ("Common Understanding and Vision") in the run-up to the WCC's 50th anniversary in 1998 and was a response to the changing ecumenical landscape at the beginning of the 21st century. The Global Christian Forum provides an open space which requires only the basic Trinitarian formula of the WCC as a common denominator. In 2013, a Theological Policy Statement declared that the sharing of faith experiences is the goal of the Forum's assemblies, in order to promote mutual knowledge, understanding and Christian community in spite of differences, and to ascertain the way the Holy Spirit is working today in the different cultures of piety.

f) Finally, it is important to highlight the consultations that have enabled an intensive exchange between WCC member churches and Pentecostal churches in recent years. A study group of the Faith and Order Commission has convened three dialogue meetings in Arusha/Tanzania (2018), Pasadena/USA (2018) and

Vitória/Brazil (2019). In the final document of the study process, special emphasis was placed on the importance of working together theologically in general. By going deeper into certain topics, new controversial positions would certainly come to light. But at the moment, it had been surprising to see how many things they had in common. The path towards a common understanding of the church was the theme at the top of the agenda.

2.4.2 Further ecumenical relations between the Pentecostal movement and other Christian churches

In addition to the efforts of the World Council of Churches to strengthen dialogue with Pentecostal churches, there are four challenges or levels of exchange within the worldwide international ecumenical movement which should be mentioned:

a) A convergence between Orthodox churches and the Pentecostal movement represents a particular challenge because of their fundamentally differing approach to liturgy and spirituality. One issue that repeatedly puts a strain on the dialogues is the mission strategy of many Pentecostal congregations and churches which make massive efforts to entice Christians of other denominations, frequently calling their theology and piety into question in the process. This practice of proselytism makes dialogue difficult in many places, especially in those regions and countries where the Orthodox Church is dominant.

b) Bilateral meetings and discussions have been taking place between the Pontifical Council for Promoting Christian Unity and representatives of the Pentecostal movement since 1972. A joint communiqué from 1976 testifies to an intensive dialogue covering many topics, above all the understanding of baptism on both sides. The long list of questions to be addressed in future dialogue is also revealing and includes many of the issues that have been discussed in all ecumenical encounters up to the present day. Since the beginning of Pope Francis' pontificate, contact with the Pentecostal movement has intensified even further. Coming as he does from Argentina, he is familiar both with the large numbers of Catholics who join the Pentecostal movement as well as with the neighbourliness practised by both sides.

c) Since 2016, the Lutheran World Federation (LWF) has been engaged internationally in an official dialogue with Pentecostal theologians and representatives of classical Pentecostal churches of a Trinitarian character. In a policy document of 2018 entitled "*Die Selbstverpflichtungen des Lutherischen Weltbundes auf dem ökumenischen Weg hin zur ekklesialen Gemeinschaft*" ("The self-commitments of the Lutheran World Federation on the ecumenical path towards ecclesial communion"), the LWF emphasises that meeting locally and understanding and appreciating each other's theological and spiritual tradition are of great importance for this dialogue with the Pentecostal movement. The Institute for Ecumenical Research in Strasbourg began to prepare the way for the Lutheran-Pentecostal dialogue in 2004. The Lutheran-Pentecostal dialogue repeatedly raises the question of the relationship between Luther's rejection of the so-called fanatics and current theological differences between Lutherans and Pentecostals.

In their self-commitment, the participants in the Lutheran-Pentecostal dialogue formulated a sentence describing a basic attitude which one might well wish for in the relations between Pentecostal churches and the EKD: "Dialogue should enable Pentecostals and Lutherans to stop repeating past prejudices, stereotypes, and misperceptions." This study document is also intended to serve this purpose.

d) The dialogue between the World Communion of Reformed Churches (WCRC) and representatives of the Pentecostal movement associated with the Pentecostal World Fellowship officially began in 1996 with a meeting at the Waldensian Church Center in Torre Pellice, Italy. Since then, three documents have been jointly adopted: *Word and Spirit, Church and World* (2000), *Experience in Christian Faith and Life: Worship, Discipleship, Discernment, Community, and Justice* (2012), and *Called to God's Mission* (2020). These three texts, published by both sides, show the positive evolution of the dialogue seen over a longer period. In the early years, a cautious rapprochement took place, with representatives of the two churches explaining themselves and setting forth basic beliefs. Better mutual understanding and growing trust led to agreement on essentials in the second document, and assumed differences were overcome or clarified. The third declaration is written in a language that shows that the understanding of mission of the two Christian communities may have different characteristics, but basically pursues the same goal and therefore welcomes joint action between the Reformed and Pentecostal churches. Representatives of both sides have expressed their desire that this dialogue would be continued.

The history of the Pentecostal movement and the more recent history of the dialogues show that the new emphasis on the work of the Spirit and the belief in the continuing revelation of God through the charismatic Christians have led to fresh thinking in the understanding of faith and the life in faith and provided the initiative for important theological debates. The Pentecostal movement is far more than a religious-sociological phenomenon; it is also a force for reformation in the literal sense of the word. In some Pentecostal churches in Africa and Latin America, the term "Second Reformation" or "alternative Reformation" is used in reference to the charismatisation of Christianity. The following third chapter aspires to enter more deeply into theological aspects of the consideration of the Pentecostal movement.

3. Theological challenges

3.1 Approaches: The Spirit at the centre

According to surveys, the Christian holiday which means the least to the Germans is Pentecost. It is apparently not even helpful to refer to the Bible text (Acts 2); on the contrary, this has an irritating effect: the fact that God is said to have poured out his Spirit on the disciples, who then spoke all at once in various languages and still understood each other, seems to many to be a beautiful story, a kind of legend, with little relevance to life today. On the other hand, in the last 20 years or so, it could be observed that students of theology with strong connections to their home churches nonetheless went fairly regularly to the services of active German Pentecostal congregations in their university towns. For a time, they "combine" these church services with their permanent connection to their home church. Clearly it is not only appealing to talk of experiencing the Holy Spirit, but more so to be assured of this experience.

In German-speaking Protestant theology, the Holy Spirit was rediscovered in the second half of the 20th century (e.g. by Jürgen Moltmann and Michael Welker). In fact, the Holy Spirit has been an essential part of the doctrine of God not only in biblical texts, but also since the time of the Early Church. This was true at the latest after 381, when the Council of Constantinople had declared the doctrine of the Trinity to be the adequate Christian expression of God's being. To be sure, this also introduced new difficulties, for example the term "person". This was actually intended to focus on God's vitality. God should not be understood (or ignored) simply as a "transcendent power" or "higher being", but as the power that shapes life in a very practical sense – in creation, in the life, cross and resurrection of Jesus, and consequently in the dynamic influence on life through God's love and justice, comfort and community formation. God's activity in creation and also in Jesus Christ were not just past events, but continued to have a concrete, ever-present and dynamic effect in all kinds of contexts in all parts of the world, and this finds its Trinitarian expression in the doctrine of the Holy Spirit. And just as is the case with the act of creation and the life of Jesus Christ, this doctrine of the Holy Spirit gains its shape through the biblical scriptures and their use of the term. As this Trinitarian idea was discovered anew, it was (re-)discovered that creation is not yet finished (creatio continua), that even before Easter the life of Jesus had been borne by the dynamism of God's Spirit, which continues to be present for us today in spite of resistance, despair and suffering. More than that: this presently experienced dynamism assures Christians that they are sent into the world as "letters of Christ" (2 Cor 3:3), so that they can feel included in the mission of the Spirit as Jesus' disciples. This affects the subjective feeling not only of being connected to God, but also of gaining life-giving power from God's Spirit, which strives towards the establishment of peace, justice and the integrity of creation with far-reaching socio-ethical implications.

⊙ Case study: Assemblies of God

The Pentecostal movement did not come out of nowhere. Its roots lie deep in the 19th century. Its antecedents include the Wesleyan Holiness Movement, Methodism and Anglicanism. In this tradition, emphasis was placed on two works of grace: salvation and sanctification. Some groups used the terms "Sanctification" and "Baptism in the Holy Spirit" synonymously. In their two-tiered theology, salvation was obtained through repentance, confession of faith and baptism. Through the subsequent experience of sanctification (baptism in the Holy Spirit), purity or perfection should be attained. These discussions continue to dominate the theological disputes that still play a role within the Pentecostal movement today.

From the beginning, there was a discussion as to whether the teaching of the New Testament sees the "baptism in the Spirit" as an experience aiming to impart purity, or as one that imbued the sanctified with power. In 1901, Charles Parham, later founder of the Apostolic Faith Movement, began to teach that the apostles' ability to speak in tongues proved their baptism in the Holy Spirit (Acts 2:4); that was how they managed to "turn the world upside down" (Acts 17:6). This became the standard opinion for almost all Pentecostal churches. The baptism in the Spirit, expressed by the ability to speak in tongues, was seen as a gift of power for a holy life. The central reference text for the understanding of the gifts of the Spirit was 1 Corinthians 12:8–10.

In the 1890 s there had been numerous revivals around the world in which many of the spiritual gifts, including speaking in tongues, had occurred. William J. Seymour preached and worked at the Azusa Street Mission in Los Angeles in the spirit of Parham's understanding of the baptism in the Spirit. He published the newspaper "The Apostolic Faith" and commissioned numerous evangelists and missionaries, so that the emerging Pentecostal doctrine spread rapidly throughout the world, connecting many awakenings that had taken place independently.

William H. Durham, an independent Baptist preacher from Chicago who had been baptised in the Spirit on Azusa Street in 1907, began to teach that sanctification was not a second, separate work of grace, but part of the "finished work" received through Christ's atoning sacrifice at Calvary. God sanctified all believers by taking them "into Christ". After this new beginning, they were to grow in sanctification or holiness. Final sanctification only came at the end of life, when believers came face to face with Christ. When Durham preached this doctrine in Azusa Street in 1911, a heated debate began that still divides the Pentecostal movement today.

The Assemblies of God were the first Pentecostal church to accept Durham's teaching. In April 1914, the "General Council" of the "Assemblies of God" came into being. Five common concerns were agreed upon: They wanted to (1) create greater unity among the various groups in the United States, (2) achieve fiscal responsibility among churches and pastors, (3) coordinate missionary efforts, (4) legalise the churches as corporate bodies, and (5) establish Bible schools and a publishing house to train and support pastors, evangelists, missionaries and lay people.

In late 1916, the Assemblies of God adopted an official theological statement, the Statement of Fundamental Truths, which contained 16 dogmatic beliefs, covering baptism and the Lord's Supper among other topics. The statement was clearly Trinitarian. While most clergy at the time used the classical Trinitarian formula for baptism according to Matthew 28:20, some held the view that one should only baptise "in the name of Jesus Christ", making reference to Acts 2:38. When the Assemblies of God officially decided on the Trinitarian formula, the proponents of a purely Jesus-based baptismal formula withdrew and formed the so-called *One-ness Movement*, a splinter group within the Pentecostal movement that attaches little or no importance to the doctrine of the Trinity. Jesus is the only point of reference in faith, in whom the Father and the Spirit work and have their being. However, a special concentration on the Son is common to all Pentecostal Christians in their practice of faith.

After the Assemblies of God had clarified their theological foundations, they invested a lot of energy in planting churches all over North America. At the same time, the army of missionaries who were to carry the Pentecostal message into the world grew. The main focus was on evangelism: people were to be brought to faith and baptised. The goal was to live a life of holiness (Rom 12:1–2), to strive for the baptism in the Spirit, which is manifested in speaking in tongues, to hold praise worship services and to receive all the gifts and callings offered by God.

The missiologist of the Assemblies of God, Melvin Hodges, adopted the "Three-Self" principle from John Nevius, the 19th century Presbyterian missionary to China. In accordance with this principle, the Assemblies of God founded indigenous churches that were *self-propagating*, *self-governing* and *self-supporting*. Although the missionary efforts of the Assemblies of God did not always succeed, they led to the founding of thousands of new churches. Today, the Assemblies of God claim 69 million members or followers worldwide. This makes them the largest Pentecostal church in the world. More than 3700 missionaries are said to be active in the mission field, and there are allegedly almost 400,000 churches. The "World Assemblies of God Fellowship" (www.worldagfellowship.org) comprises 144 self-governing councils, each representing a national church body. Many of these groups are also members of the Pentecostal World Fellowship and the World Evangelical Alliance.

At the same time the significance of the Holy Spirit was discovered within Protestant theology in the 20th century, Pentecostal congregations were growing, especially in the churches of the Global South. Their focus lies on the present experience of God as the Holy Spirit. It can be seen that an internal theological discourse is taking place within the diversity of the worldwide Pentecostal movement, its concrete congregations and churches, and especially in academic Pentecostal theology. There is definitely controversy among Pentecostals about certain emphases and consequences of the general theology of the Holy Spirit attempted above, and this also applies to confessional theology in Germany, which is characterised by historical typologies. One example concerns the accusation levelled during the Reformation at the Anabaptist movement of the time that it was striving for an ideal of moral perfection by invoking the presence of the Holy Spirit; now it is debated whether this is true in this generalised form. There is no doubt, however, that this prejudice still influences the fundamentally sceptical perception of the German regional churches towards free church and Pentecostal piety today.

Another topic of discussion is the direct spiritual experience supposedly demonstrated by Pentecostal piety. In the Reformation period, the followers of the Anabaptist movement who were pneumatically moved were critically labelled "fanatics" because their experience of the Spirit served their subjectivist self-interest, irrespective of biblical testimony or the revelation received in Christ. This accusation can however hardly be upheld today, since it has been recognised that the Reformation leaders had a very biased interpretation of Anabaptist theology – a most important facet of their involvement in the deadly persecution of the Anabaptist followers. Nonetheless, the theological formula – namely that the effects of the Spirit could not be perceived as such independently of the "Word" – still serves frequently as a criterion for the theological legitimacy of Pentecostal Spirit-piety today. This belief has long been accepted in academic Pentecostal theology, both among representatives of German Pentecostal churches[16] and in global Pentecostal theology[17], and is thoroughly developed here theologically and exegetically. The Spirit experienced by the believers must be able to be understood as the Spirit of the exalted Christ. In this discourse a complex theology of experience emerges, which takes into account the interpretation and imagination of the subjects of this experience (cf. chapter 3.2). Nevertheless, with regard to the Pentecostal movement, as in all forms of church life in the past and present, it is necessary to assume that there are all kinds of devotional practice of varying complexity and reflection. This consideration already played a role in the debate with Pietism in the academic theology of the 19th century (e.g. Albrecht Ritschl).

In Reformation theology, we know the doctrine of the Holy Spirit above all as the doctrine of the divine "attraction" that draws people into faith. This means that Christian faith is not primarily the result of a good Christian upbringing, Sunday school teaching or religious education at school, but is principally the result of God's "attraction" and enlightenment as one

---

16 See the thematic issue of *Ökumenische Rundschau* 3/2011: „Pfingstkirchen in der Ökumene" and *Evangelische Theologie* issue 4/2009.
17 See the bibliography e.g. the works of *Archer* 2004, *Yong* 2002, *Macchia* 2010.

understands the gospel. This is expressed in the *Lutheran conception of faith as a gift of the Holy Spirit* as well as with *Calvin's doctrine of the inward testimony of the Holy Spirit.* The Reformation approaches can certainly be connected with the Pentecostal emphasis on the *experience* of the Holy Spirit, as long as one avoids a trivial view of the verbal inspiration (that biblical texts are exactly inspired by the Spirit). It is only if the effect of the Spirit is understood as the *linkage* of personal experience, the Word that is preached and the context in the congregation that the idea of scriptural inspiration does not appear trivial. There is also reference to this kind of connection in the discussion which is partly held within the Pentecostal churches concerning the supposed immediacy of the Spirit's effect.

The link between personal experience, the preaching and the local (congregational) context relates well to the modern understanding of experience with which we are familiar, at least in Europe, since the advent of the modern age. There is a general awareness that no experience is possible unless it is conveyed by human culture. The subjects of any experience are influenced by certain basic assumptions and notional frameworks shaped by history and culture, and are thus always involved in the formation of their experience. The idea of an inner space of pure experiential immediacy is therefore fiction. It is thus impossible to distinguish clearly between experience of the human spirit and the divine spirit.

From a Reformation perspective and with respect to the correlation outlined above, the effect of the Holy Spirit as a renewing force of faith can also lead to a concept of "sanctification", above all as growth in love. The so-called radical wing of the Reformation drew social-ethical consequences in this context and determined to follow the Sermon on the Mount rigidly in ethical matters. This close connection between faith and ethics certainly represented a shift in emphasis compared to Luther. In the centuries that followed, such concepts were adopted by various holiness movements and connected with enthusiastic experiences of being seized by the Spirit. As a result, the doctrine of "baptism in the Spirit" has become characteristic of Pentecostal Christianity. According to this doctrine, one recognises either the initial establishment of the relationship with God or its confirmation and deepening through an intensive experience of being filled with the Holy Spirit (in the form of speaking in tongues or in other forms). Another dispute among Pentecostals concerns the interpretation of the so-called "prosperity Christianity", according to which the presence of the Spirit is demonstrated by the believers' economic success, which is promised in the mission (→ Prosperity gospel). Academic theology continues to debate whether the enthusiastic experience of being seized by the Spirit should be regarded as a prerequisite for "true Christianity" or whether it is not an expression of a certain kind of devotional piety. In the Lutheran tradition, the enlightenment through the Spirit, imparting the gifts of faith and love, is regarded as an almost imperceptible process, both as an inward experience and in its outward appearance. That is not sufficient for the followers of the Pentecostal movement. When it comes to an exchange of views, members of the regional Protestant churches will have to be prepared to be asked how their Christian faith is recognisable.

The following subsections of this chapter develop individual aspects of Pentecostal theology regarding the concrete experience of God's presence as the Holy Spirit. They are intended to prepare the ground for possible talks between local congregations. Pentecostal theology of the Spirit can be briefly characterised in three key focus areas, which also designate the subchapters in this section:

- The Spirit of God is associated with an *appreciation of diversity*. This involves a fundamental analysis of the Pauline doctrine of charisms (1 Cor 12) and of the concept of experience already mentioned above. In their internal discussion, Pentecostals argue against exclusivist tendencies in the understanding of spiritual gifts.[18] (Cf. Chap. 3.2 Experience, 3.3 Scripture, 3.8 Empowerment and 3.10 Charisma and Authority).
- The connection between Christology and the experience of the Spirit is based above all on an emphasis on the *certainty of redemption*. The theology of healing also belongs in this area. (Cf. chap. 3.5 Christology, 3.6 Eschatology, 3.8 Prayer/Healing and 3.9 Music and Praise). This focus is going through a particular development in dealing with human disabilities. Since the Pentecostal theologian Amos Yong published "Theology and Down Syndrome" in 2007, there has been a lively discussion on this topic. The combination of Christology, pneumatology and eschatology also forms the background to Pentecostal political theology in the sense of liberation theology.
- Hoping for the presence of the Spirit is closely connected with *hope for a surprising change*. Pentecostal theology develops corresponding philosophical and theological concepts in association with the sciences (cf. chap. 3.4 Creation). This is combined with an interest in a theology emphasising the mission (and dynamism) of God (cf. chap. 3.11 Mission and 3.12 Unity and Ecumenism).

---

18 See *Fee* 2014, *Yong* 2014.

The following sections of this chapter unfold various theological aspects of Pentecostal theology and propose topics and questions which can play a role in interdenominational conversations with Pentecostal groups and congregations. The titles of the sub-chapters contain a thesis introduced by "We...". This common proposition including Pentecostal attitudes is suggested as the starting point of a mutual dialogue.

3.2 What happens to us: The significance of experience

Experience plays a central role in Pentecostal faith. And without the concept of experience traditional Protestant theology is also incomplete. The Reformation would not have been possible without the experience of justification by faith alone. For the Reformer Martin Luther, a theology without experience was unthinkable; indeed, it is experience that makes the theologian. Even the study of the Holy Scriptures is not purely a matter of the intellect but, according to Luther, requires *oratio* (prayer), *meditatio* (meditation) and *tentatio* (temptation).

Nonetheless, 30 years ago, if a student of Protestant theology had referred to their experience – possibly even conversion – and cited it as a source of knowledge and reassurance, they could well have been warned during a seminar on exegesis that they should keep their personal faith separate from academic reflection. In those days, this did not only apply to those who were "pious", but also to others, whether students or teachers, who were keen readers of liberation theology and stressed the experience of oppression and liberation.

The basic assumption of the opponents of experience was that *rationality* was more important than experience and enthusiasm, especially when it came to affect the body directly. But this scepticism about experience is gradually giving way to the realisation that for many people today strong sensory impressions and physical experiences sometimes represent the epitome of an intensive and thus meaningful life, and that "rational religion" is more a construct of modern times than a proprium of Christian identity. Apart from that, experience does not necessarily mean something unreasonable or irrational. In the Protestant theological tradition – and naturally in the Catholic tradition, too – there are famous advocates of a theology of experience: Friedrich Schleiermacher and Paul Althaus, for example, or Dorothee Sölle with her emphasis on the interrelation of mysticism and resistance. Currently, the number of publications on aesthetics in the Aristotelian sense of sensual perception and interpretation is increasing – in theology as well. And the recent supplements to the Protestant hymnals of the German regional churches show that the landscape is changing rapidly here, too. Contemporary worship songs are no longer automatically suspected of manipulating religious feelings.

In this context, Pentecostal spirituality, which is strongly oriented towards emotional and bodily experiences, is also gaining importance in ecumenical discourse. The aforementioned development towards a greater inclusion of experiential practices, which also occurs within the historical churches, does not prevent the continued irritation caused by individual, especially bodily experiences of speaking in tongues, baptism in the Spirit, healing and deliverance from demonic possession, as is felt by church members, theologians or even practised ecumenists. A central reason for this is probably the interpretation of these experiences. Pentecostal Christians interpret them as signs of the immediate working of the Holy Spirit – not simply as a state of religious or emotional excitement. The decisive question for ecumenical dialogue is therefore not so much *whether* the Spirit of God causes experience, but *what kind* and *how*. Parallels and commonalities do emerge in this regard between Pentecostal churches and historical Protestant churches.

So how can experiences that come from God's Spirit be distinguished from other general human or religious experiences? The Pentecostals have answered this question theologically in various ways. They all acknowledge that they do not intend to make a sweeping new theological qualification of religious experience or a justification of piety that is fundamentally based on experience and characterised, for example, by particularly intensive conversion events. The special aspect of Pentecostal piety and theology is rather to be found in the way that it sees specific experiences as the immediate working of the Holy Spirit, for most Pentecostal theologians agree that experiences in the Spirit are a form of revelation (Terry L. Cross). Experiences such as speaking in tongues, trance or healing are attributed to the working of divine spiritual power. For Pentecostal theology, it is important that experiences in the Spirit are not taken to be natural experiences, for they are considered to be supernatural and therefore unable to be influenced or controlled by human beings. For this reason, such spiritual experiences are also called passions, because they cause something to occur to the human. Others use the term "affect" in order to make it clear that the experience in the Spirit is direct and spontaneous, independent of any reflection or knowledge, and also of any personal state of emotion (Wolfgang Vondey).

Because of this experiential and affective nature, religious scholars such as Paul Jenkins or Samuel Huntington ascribe an anti-intellectual tendency to Pentecostal churches – especially those of the Global South; sometimes they even depict an almost segregationist vision of growing irrational religiosity that will overrun the Global North from the Global South. But this ascription is untenable, also with regard to Pentecostal theologies. The question of the quality of Spirit experiences is treated with strong differentiation among Pentecostal theologies, so that the ball is rather in the other court, posing theological considerations that can best be dealt with in depth in dialogue. The Pentecostal theologian Wolfgang Vondey postulates that Pentecostal emotions and experiences bring Pentecostal theology to the limits of its linguistic, theoretical, conceptual and systematic possibilities. Of course, this does not only apply to Pentecostal or charismatic experiences, but to religious experiences in general and to a multitude of other experiences. Vondey's observation thus rather stimulates fundamental questions. How far can experiences be translated into language? Is there not always an excess, something more that cannot be sorted into intellectual, rational categories of interpretation? An experience that eludes rationalisation and thus lies outside the project of modernity is still considered offensive, alarming, irrational. That goes for the Protestant Church as well, which for centuries has understood itself as the church of the word and of enlightenment and cultivates a spirituality that is principally marked by intellect and knowledge. Protestant theology, especially in the northern hemisphere, does indeed assume that the Spirit is immanently present and active in the world, but rather in a still, small voice and silent prayer than "as an omnipotent and alien mystery that miraculously breaks in with the rush of a great, strong wind" (Frank Macchia).

For the ecumenical dialogue and cooperation between Pentecostal and Protestant churches, it is important not to reduce the differences described above to an opposition between reason and experience, playing them off against one another. It is rather a matter of rediscovering the importance of experience in traditional Protestant theology and piety and of de-mythologising the assumption that the Spirit is invisible or unable to be directly experienced, which has almost taken on dogmatic traits.

The aspect emphasised by Pentecostal theologians, that humans are passive and the Spirit is active, aligns well with the Reformation teaching of the various "soli". On the other hand, one should be wary of setting any conditions, whether it be the requirement of particular spiritual experiences as proof of authenticity, the demand for a certain conversion experience or for a certain degree of cognitive insight into the contents of the Christian faith.

When it comes to the discernment of spirits, it is less important whether this is done by means of reason or spirit-worked emotions. It is more important to know whether it is the Spirit of God who is manifested in lowliness and weakness, in suffering and sympathy, and who opposes the mighty and all forms of triumphalism. With regard to speaking in tongues, Pentecostal theologians have moved onward in this direction and do not see this gift in a triumphalist sense as a sign of special election, but as a sign of the presence of God and the Holy Spirit in immanent lowliness and weakness.

The search for a common basis and for points of contact for ecumenical dialogue must and should not level out the particularities of the individual approaches. Some researchers right-ly point out that Pentecostal spirituality based on experience and bodily happenings leads at the same time to a change in the knowledge about God, the perception of God and the re-lationship to God. Experiential spirituality, which ranges from emotional prayer to trance states and exorcisms, is acquired in a learning process and is veritably trained (Tanja Luhrmann). Words no longer play a central role. Rather, body and senses are directly involved in the acquisition of knowledge. Rituals and psychological techniques are not only tools, but play the central part in spirituality. Knowledge acquired physically be-comes more significant than in historical Protestant churches or even in free churches in the West. The result of this acquired behaviour is that many Pentecostals claim to have an intimate relationship with God.

Ultimately, the Pentecostal accent on experience is thus con-nected with the emphasis on another bodily form of knowledge about God that goes beyond cognition and on a different form of knowledge acquisition. In the history of the church, there are also precursors for these forms of knowing God and relating to God, although they play a mostly marginal role, for example in mysticism or in the various revivalist movements from Mon-tanism to Pietism. However, this does not stand in the way of rediscovering religious experience in the body, interpreting and reflecting it theologically against the background of modern life experiences and the search for meaning. For it is characteristic for our modern high-tech world on the one hand that everyday life is increasingly dematerialised and disembodied, so that the body is forced out. This trend was pushed forward decisively in modern times by the processes of social differentiation and division of labour and progresses today in the development of artificial intelligence and robotics. On the other hand, the body, including physically experienced religiosity (in yoga, pilgrimage, etc.), is receiving more attention than ever before. The body is highly valued and kept fit until old age. The belief in the perfect body and intense bodily experiences becomes in some cases the final instance for meaning and experience. Can there be a connection here: on the one hand, body optimisation and the maximisation of the sense of bodily experiences; on the other, the radical decline of belief in a bodily resurrection and thus in the resurrection body? This would be just one of the many theologically and socially relevant questions that would be worth discussing with representatives of Pentecostal churches.

3.3 What guides us: The understanding of scripture

What should the attitude of Christians be to the Bible? What standards guide them in their reading and study of the biblical scriptures? Does scripture have a centre, from which the different statements of the Bible can be assessed? Is the Bible God's Word, or is it contained within it?

It is known that Luther demanded that all biblical books be judged according to whether they "inculcate Christ or not". Furthermore, he criticised the Epistle of James as an "epistle of straw" because it only speaks generally of faith in God without any mention of Jesus' passion and resurrection (WA DB VII 385) and even makes a positive connection between faith and works. As a consequence of these remarks, Protestants disagree about the appropriate understanding and interpretation of the Bible.

In recent decades, a number of renowned Pentecostal scholars have begun practicing and reflecting on Pentecostal exegesis and hermeneutics, using scientific methods as a matter of course. Their research should stand in comparison with that of non-Pentecostal scholars. In his foreword to the "Handbook of Pentecostal and Charismatic Theology,"[19] published in 2014, Michael Bergunder, Professor of Religious Studies and Intercultural Theology in Heidelberg, therefore explicitly rejects the allegation that the worldwide Pentecostal movement has no theology corresponding to that of the established churches.

At the same time, Bergunder points out that the Pentecostal movement in Germany has hardly accepted this. Apart from recognising the (literal) inspiration of the Bible, they hold to the two central concepts of "infallibility" and "absolute inerrancy" of the Bible. These in turn are connected with the development of a history of salvation, the understanding of which is of decisive importance when weighing individual biblical statements. One of the founders of this interpretation of salvation history in the Bible is John Nelson Darby, whose model of dispensationalism had a great influence on American → fundamentalism from the 19th century. This model assumes that the sequence of historical periods follows a distribution determined by God (so-called *dispensation*) and that its regularities can be followed in the Bible texts.

The Pentecostal movement which emerged at the turn of the 19th and 20th centuries was never actually part of this fundamentalism. Nevertheless, it shares a number of its convictions, such as the belief in the direct inspiration of the biblical books

---

19 See *Haustein/Maltese* 2014.

and the presupposition of a history of salvation, which became the standard for interpreting the Bible. The Pentecostal movement's view of salvation history is not pessimistic. In Germany, the Pentecostal movement emerged in the context of the Fellowship movement, founded on the Evangelical Alliance of 1846 (now the German *Evangelische Allianz*). After several conferences at the beginning of the 20th century, which were marked by speaking in tongues and other manifestations of the Spirit, large parts of the Fellowship movement and also some free-church representatives of the Evangelical Alliance distanced themselves from the Pentecostal believers in 1909 with the so-called → "Berlin Declaration" (see chapter 2.1). Despite agreeing on the Bible and mostly also on biblical hermeneutics, their differences regarding the working of the Spirit and the baptism in the Spirit were sufficient for them to label the new movement as "from below" and satanic.

This delimitation continued to determine the relationship between the fellowship or Alliance movements and the Pentecostals for decades and led repeatedly to mutual denigrations. Then, in 1996, there was a "Joint Declaration of the Board of the German Evangelical Alliance (DEA) and the Executive Committee of the Association of Pentecostal Churches (BFP)". In this declaration, the BFP committed itself to the principles of the Evangelical Alliance. With regard to the doctrine of the Holy Spirit and the practice of the gifts of the Spirit, one of the points jointly confessed was that the emphatic agreements did not allow for an understanding of various stages of salvation. While the DEA could see this as a renunciation of the doctrine of the baptism of the Spirit as a second blessing, it signified for the BFP a reassurance of the position of "Finished Work Pentecostalism", which had developed within the Pentecostal movement since 1910. This regarded baptism in the Spirit as a confirmation of conversion and not as a substantial complementary addition.

This agreement does not include those Pentecostal groups known as the ☉ "Church of God". They consider the baptism in the Spirit to be an independent second blessing on the converts. The joint declaration of DEA and BFP was so openly formulated that neither side had to renounce their respective doctrinal commitments. The result was a phase of strengthened cooperation between Pentecostal and non-Pentecostal groups within the framework of local and regional Evangelical Alliances. Due to the joint rejection of supernatural phenomena, such as "resting in the Spirit" or casting out so-called "territorial spirits", this cooperation only referred to those BFP congregations with classical Pentecostal theology and piety.

The Pentecostal-charismatic currents that had taken root in Germany since the 1960 s and 1970 s were thus explicitly rejected. They had begun during a Pentecostal renewal movement in the 1940 s in Canada which became known as the "New Order of the Latter Rain" or Latter Rain Movement. This movement was very close to the healing movement that was active at the same time and combined the experience of healing with the defence against or deliverance from demonic forces. From the 1960 s onwards, healing meetings were also held in Germany, supported and financed by Pentecostal organisations (e.g. the "Full Gospel Business Men's Fellowship"). This led to the foundation of some scattered neo-Pentecostal congregations and then from the 1970 s and 80 s to a stronger network of such centres. They shared the scriptural understanding of the classical Pentecostal movement, believing in the (literal) inspiration of the Bible, and in the early years also held to the doctrine of the baptism in the Spirit. However, other than the Pentecostal movement, they did not see sanctification as the prerequisite for receiving this baptism, but rather deliverance from demonic oppressions. Thus the doctrine of the baptism in the Spirit moved into the background; the idea of the manifestations of the Spirit (see below) came to the fore instead, alongside the so-called deliverance ministry. It became a kind of trademark for the neo- Pentecostal movement.

As from the mid-1980s, this was followed by another movement which, as a successor to Pentecostalism and the Charismatic movement, called itself the "Third Wave of the Holy Spirit" and explicitly rejected the doctrine of the baptism of the Spirit. The goal of its founder and long-time leader John Wimber was evangelism with signs and wonders.

Wimber's fundamental scriptural hermeneutic, from which he derives his specifically Pentecostal concept of evangelism, is founded on the broad stream of tradition initiated by the development of the historical-critical method in the second half of the 19th century. In the meantime, both historical criticism and evangelical or fundamentalist anti-criticism are assigned to the same positivist scientific ideal. However, this ideal has become less significant since the 1950s. Instead, a variety of approaches to analysing and understanding the biblical texts has emerged, so that some of the differences in theological training between universities and free-church seminaries have diminished. Historical criticism is not automatically seen to invalidate the fundamental importance of the Bible for the formation and development of faith. Academic theology is open to hermeneutical approaches based on the final canonical form of the biblical text. One unifying element is the assumption that the biblical texts can in every case be seen as an expression of faith by people who have had personal experiences of God whose effect goes beyond the individual. The theological designation of the Bible as "God's Word" is to be seen increasingly in this context and not only against the background of interpretational methods.

Luther's conviction that Scripture interprets itself by proclaiming Christ thus receives the framework which Luther regarded as self-evident, long before the discovery of historical criticism: that the Bible, read in the community of believers, is the binding basis of faith.

3.4 What is all around us: God's work in creation

At first glance, it appears obvious what Christians mean by creation: they acknowledge the primordial connection between God and the world. "God made the world" means that we owe the life-giving foundations of the world to God, whom we therefore call Creator. This also implies that we bear the responsibility for these life-giving foundations, as has been emphasised in an ecological doctrine of creation, especially in recent decades. For many people this means that the concept of creation refers particularly to the sensory experience of nature as a whole and in its various parts – although the Christian understanding of creation does not stop there, but also includes, for example, social and ethical conditions such as justice and peace. The Christian belief in creation includes an interest in a theory of the *origin of the world*, but also focuses on the more practical question – partly ethical, partly spiritual – of how to *shape the relationship* between creature and Creator and between creatures.

In traditional creation theology, questions of knowledge and piety are dovetailed against this background. This plays a major role in the discussion with Pentecostal theology of creation. For here, interestingly, the topic of creation hardly appears in the theoretical problem of how the world came into being. Rather, the Pentecostal experience of the *redeeming* effect of the Holy Spirit is the starting point for considerations on creation. Taken from this viewpoint, the working of the Spirit extends to the entire breadth of nature that can be experienced by the senses.

However, this is exactly the topic which has been debated in confessional theology for centuries: can we really recognise the working of the Spirit so precisely empirically and physically? In the 19th century, Friedrich Schleiermacher opposed the so-called "supernaturalism", which saw the working of God as a "supernatural working". Modern theology was concerned that this could stir up "superstitious" tendencies. In Reformation times, there had already been attempts to curb such tendencies by a strong emphasis on the Bible and Christ. They preferred to focus on the reference to Jesus Christ, rather than on the independent working of the Spirit. This discourse finds its continuation in the current Pentecostal theology of creation: could Christians not also be surprised by the Spirit's working, something going beyond the limits and laws of nature and physics? Do we not all put our trust in this when we say a prayer at the bedside of someone who is seriously ill – even if we dare not hope for a literal fulfilment? Maybe it was the hope that God could overcome natural boundaries which motivated the "supernaturalists". Does the presumption that such an effect is possible really have to stand in contradiction to the findings of modern medicine, biology or physics? Interestingly, these questions about the Christian understanding of reality also lead back to considerations about theories of the origin of the world. They encourage us to overcome the stalemate between nature and the supernatural through a concept of creation that is based on the redeeming (and breaking boundaries) experience of the Spirit.

The belief in creation is thereby more closely linked to the belief in redemption than was the case in classical theology. God's creation is already sustained by his redeeming Spirit, and therefore the experience of redemption by the Spirit is not granted to an elite group with particularly spiritual gifts. On the contrary, the effects of the Spirit can overcome barriers of race and class. This would be an example of how the redemptive working of the Spirit strengthens the social nature of humanity. Speaking in tongues (→ glossolalia) and healing of the sick, central elements of worship in Pentecostalism (especially in the Global South), are symbols (or even sacraments?) of a bodily nature of human life oriented towards God. Pentecostal theology invites us to understand spirit and nature not as opposites, but in a holistic way, so that the idea of creation increasingly serves this purpose. Do not the experiences of glossolalia and spiritual healing demonstrate that God's Spirit brings about redemption in all dimensions of creation?

In this context, academic Pentecostal theology is working on a holistic theory of reality that could also enter into discourse with the natural sciences. "*Emergence*" is the guiding concept here. The term is based on a specific understanding of spirit and indicates an organisational structure of reality that is not totally different from material nature, but more complex. For example, this structure is not bound by the barriers of space and time (one example would be one's thoughts). Above all, it can *emerge* under certain, but not precisely predictable natural conditions (surprisingly and beyond limitations). It can thus lead to a reaction in the less complex, natural organisation of the world. Because of this so-called downward causation, the Spirit cannot be replaced and made superfluous during the course of evolution by a more complex form of natural organisation. Thus, in Pentecostal thinking on creation, it can be said that God continues to act in, on and with creation through his Spirit. References to the biblical concept of the creation of the world can easily be found: Genesis 1:2 ff., for example, already speaks of the work of the divine Spirit hovering over the primeval waters. Pentecostal authors such as Amos Yong see this as an image of levels of reality lying over and building upon one another. This allows the emergence theories to explain the appearance of spirit in nature combined with a uniform (monistic) overall concept of reality.

These theological concepts of creation can be significant when reflecting on the Christian creation belief. They make it possible to think of creation without the image of a personal God, an image which vexes a considerable number of church members, as has been shown both by the most recent membership surveys of the EKD and by studies concerning religious education. Here is an opportunity to reflect on belief together with Pentecostal theologies. Essentially, the theory of emergence describes biological, chemical and physical forms of organisation of reality and does not suggest the concept of persons, who by nature are supposed to be more than, yet different from, organisms. Emergence is fundamentally a monistic concept that rejects the dualism of spirit and nature. This conforms very well to the Pentecostal redemption experience, in which God's Spirit addresses all areas of creation in a holistic way; personal concepts are subordinated to this.

Closer consideration of this approach could also show what might possibly be lost by the concept of a personal God who creates the world by deliberate action and then directs his attention to it in compassion and righteousness, and why the classical doctrine of creation in confessional churches is mainly shaped in a personalised fashion. Is it not so that the dignity of humans can be justified more explicitly with a personal creator God? For if God, who is himself a person, creates human beings in his image, they too must be recognised and treated as persons. The question is also whether the concept of a personal creator does not also make it easier to differentiate clearly between creator and creature, something which we do not want to abandon.

Whatever may come out of a concrete conversation regarding our belief in this matter, it is clear that it is only at first glance that one might gain the impression that confessional and Pentecostal theologies of creation contradict each other. The strong emphasis on personalisation on the one hand appears to be opposed to a holistic way of thinking on the other. But these contradictory impressions are put into perspective when one considers the respective approaches. The creation doctrine of the traditional denominations is interested in the origin of the world in God; Pentecostal creation theology is based entirely on redemption experienced through particular workings of the Spirit, and assumes that these must also underlie creation. By taking these differing approaches into account, it is possible to discover significant similarities in both traditions.

The holistic interest shown by the Pentecostal theology of creation is also increasingly considered to be a valid concern by the traditional denominational churches. It was only during the

Reformation that it was distorted by the focus of all theology on personal redemption. The personal contrast between Creator and creature, however, does not imply a dualism in creation theology that throws the original goodness of creation into question because the creatures contradict the Creator. Indeed, the theologies of the traditional denominations also affirm the unity of spirit and nature, which can be described in Pentecostalism in the shape of the emergence theory. Pentecostal theologies, for their part, see the whole of creation as filled with the Holy Spirit, but they do not deny that the creatures have created an unholy distance from the Spirit; they can certainly acknowledge that creation is dependent on redemption through God's sanctifying Spirit.

3.5 When we devote ourselves: Christ as Lord and Saviour

Would it be easier for Christians to communicate their faith if they could simply say outright that Jesus was just a prophet? It is certainly difficult to communicate the position of classical Christology, which ascribes to him a divine "added value", argues that he had both divine and human nature, and even understands him to be in some way identical with God (albeit considered in terms of a Trinitarian differentiation). It may well be assumed that not only the majority of Protestant church members, but also the majority of pastors would be quite content with a so-called "low" Christology, which would allow them to speak of Jesus as a prophet endowed with the Spirit. The results of a survey from 2014 covering the situation of the Roman Catholic and Protestant churches in the German state of Hesse at that time confirms this claim: 22 percent of the Roman

Catholics and 33 percent of the Protestants did not agree with the statement that there is a God who has revealed himself in Christ.[20] The authors of the study see this as an indication that one could speak of a "Christianity without Christ" in Germany. The theologian Michael Welker observes the tendency for Jesus Christ to be seen as a "cultural factor", somehow omnipresent, in such a way that " that people have become accustomed to him – like the church in the village".[21]

In the midst of these difficulties with Christology, we now observe how Pentecostal and charismatic believers are touched in a completely new way by the real experience of the Spirit of God and the tangible presence of Jesus Christ. Perhaps it is not so much the spectacular signs of the presence of the Spirit – sometimes known as "special experiences" – which can pose a provocative challenge to Christians in the established churches. It may rather be the certainty displayed by Pentecostal and charismatic congregations that they feel the absolutely genuine and concrete presence of Jesus. This has had a disconcerting effect on mainstream church culture. Perhaps we are unsettled to discover that for them God is clearly more than just an old village church.

This could be a reminder that faith in Jesus Christ is faith in the *present* Christ, the *Christus praesens*. Pentecostal theology begins with a holistic experience of God as a redemptive experience and is thus frequently confronted with the sceptical question of whether the "heart" of the Christian faith, the person of Jesus Christ including the historical Jesus, actually plays a

---

20 *Michael N. Eberz*, Was glauben die Hessen? Ergebnisse einer Umfrage im Auftrag des Hessischen Rundfunks, in: ebd./Meinhard Schmidt-Degenhard (eds.), Was glauben die Hessen? Horizonte religiösen Lebens, Berlin 2014, 11–85; esp. 75.
21 *Michael Welker*, Gottes Offenbarung. Christologie, Neukirchen-Vluyn 2012, 28.

subordinate role in its thinking. Such scepticism usually provokes fierce rejoinders. After all, Jesus is the original bearer of the Spirit. The work of the biblical Jesus in releasing people from demons is a topic of discussion in Bible study groups that are well attended and try to relate the stories to their own situation. Seen in this way, every sensory experience of the Spirit in the past and hoped for in the future is a kind of divine confirmation that Jesus' redeeming work is active in the present. In this sense, Pentecostal Christology even gives strong support for a Trinitarian understanding of redemption, thus placing it alongside a major theological development after the Second World War.

In the confrontation with the political ideologies of the 20th century, it was important to speak of the "Lord" Jesus Christ as resistance to political claims to power. This entailed the risk of a Christomonism that neglected the pneumatological dimension of the Christian faith. The fact that Jesus Christ must not only be regarded as a person "endowed with the Spirit", but is also himself present in the Spirit (and by all means also critical of the church), came into the focus of theology after 1960 with the catchword "Spirit Christology". A more deliberate Trinitarian connection between reflections on Christ and on the Spirit enables Christ's redemptive work to be replenished with guidance from the "case studies" taken from the Bible: the establishment of peace and justice, of healing and of sanctification. Here there are many opportunities for contact and discussion with Pentecostal Christianity in order to search jointly for the content of the Christian promise of salvation.

However, one should not imagine that Pentecostal theologians who understand salvation as described above as only viewing it as an alternative model to the traditional Christology of the confessional churches. They are indeed involved in their own inner-Pentecostal debates. The Trinitarian understanding of salvation is a major point of contention within the Pentecostal movement with regard to the so-called *oneness Pentecostals*. This minority, which is quite strong in Pentecostalism worldwide, affirms a faith that does not follow the distinctions of the doctrine of the Trinity. In dialogue with this group, the explicit correlation between Christology and pneumatology cannot be a meaningful goal.

Pentecostal piety and theology place redemption at the centre of Christology, but this is not meant in a triumphalist sense. Nor does it justify the assumption that this is at the expense of the person of the Redeemer. The Pentecostal *Foursquare movement*, for example, speaks of the four pillars of its Christianity: evangelistic preaching, baptism in the Spirit, healing and servant leadership. It traces them back to Jesus as Saviour, Baptiser with the Holy Spirit, Healer and Coming King. Pentecostal impulses such as these have spawned a Christological reflection on the person of Christ across group boundaries in Pentecostalism. The fundamental insight is that in the light of the prophecy made by John the Baptist according to the biblical accounts, the life and death of Jesus Christ appear to be a story of significance when taken in context: "He will baptise you with the Holy Spirit and with fire" (Matt 3:11). Thus, while Jesus himself receives the baptism of Spirit and fire in his death on the cross, his resurrection makes him the one who then administers this baptism. The patterns of thought developed in these elaborated Pentecostal Christologies are clearly different from those of the traditional confessional Christologies, but can still be methodically conveyed, for they can be read as a corrective to established forms of Christological doctrine that make a distinction between the person and work of Christ.

Naturally, the Pentecostal topic of salvation through the Spirit of Jesus Christ ranges much further than has been articulated so far, even much wider than has yet been covered within contemporary academic Pentecostal theories. In significant areas of worldwide Pentecostalism, there is a concrete belief that God's Spirit of redemption can only be experienced after this redeeming Spirit has overcome other spirits known and recognised as evil. In many African cultures, this idea is inherent in the indigenous religiosity with which Pentecostal Christianity coexists and competes, and it influences the religious form, whether in the mission churches or independent, indigenous African types of Christianity. Admittedly, even in our own present-day culture, with bestsellers such as "Harry Potter", "The Lord of the Rings" or "Star Wars", we can detect a (new?) preference for a mythological struggle of good against evil. Be that as it may – from a Pentecostal point of view and against this background, redemption can only mean redemption from evil. In these Pentecostal Christologies, the experience of the Spirit must be linked to the "testing of the spirits" (after 1 John 4:1 ff.).

Walter Hollenweger (1997) points out that the Methodist Holiness Movement exercised a historical influence on parts of the worldwide Pentecostal movement. Classical Methodism emphasised the necessity of sanctification in the lives of believers and presented it as the victory of good over evil, because it was the overcoming of sin in earthly life. The idea that believers were born again to a new life forms a biblical basis for this view (cf. Jn 3:3, 5). The idea of *spiritual warfare*, which is characteristic in many places for Pentecostal piety calling itself *born again Christianity*, corresponds to this idea of sanctification, even if a historical connection to Methodism cannot be assumed in all cases. The reference to the Holiness Movement is nonetheless important. It helps to explain that there can be a smooth transition from the claim for a testing of the spirits to a → *prosperity gospel*, which interprets victory against the evil spirits socio-economically. Together with Pentecostal congregations, it would be necessary to discuss jointly how the participants in the conversation understand the hope of salvation and healing in their lives and why some might quite consciously prefer to develop less concrete ideas.

3.6 What is in store for us: Eschatology and apocalypticism

Christians outside the Pentecostal movement often find that the eschatology is its most striking, even alarming feature. Pentecostals speculate about the end of the world, they spread disconcerting fantasies about the "rapture" and the "tribulation" as well as wild predictions about the return of Jesus, which their preachers continue to propound in spite of numerous refutations and unfulfilled prophecies.

One ought, however, to put these impressions into a wider context. From the very beginning, Jesus' followers were puzzled by the delay of his return in glory. In 1 Thessalonians, his oldest surviving letter, the Apostle Paul is obviously convinced that Jesus will return during his lifetime. On the other hand, in his last letter, Romans, he argues that the mission to the Gentiles is so important that God is deliberately delaying the faith of the Jews in order to gather the nations.

This was the line of thinking that was also followed later. Patristic authors such as Justin Martyr and Irenaeus speculated on the last days with the help of the Book of Revelation. The medieval theologian Joachim of Fiore described the three ages of the Father, the Son and the Holy Spirit. Luther and other important reformers could hardly imagine that the world would go on in face of the violent turmoils that accompanied the Reformation. Even a classical pietist like Johann Albrecht Bengel predicted an exact date for Christ's return in 1836, and even though Johann Christoph Blumhardt and his son Christoph Friedrich Blumhardt ultimately rejected a precise date for the return of Christ, an increased expectation of the Kingdom of God in the near future was a central element of their influential of preaching and healing.

So this is the point: looking at the whole of church history, the Pentecostals are by no means peculiar or unusual in their emphasis on eschatology. The American environment which gave rise to the → Azusa Street Revival, generally regarded as the starting point for what we now call the Pentecostal movement, was full of apocalyptic and premillenarianist expectations. Some of these were decades older than Azusa. The emergence of a new nation and a new beginning, freed from the baggage of state churches and European history, contributed to the basic feeling of living in exciting times.

What distinguished the Pentecostal movement from the unfulfilled prophecies such as those of the Adventists or Jehovah's Witnesses? What led to the growth of hope of the "Coming King" (one of the four principles of the *Foursquare movement*) where so many other hopes withered away?

It seems that the combination of two factors played a role in placing eschatology at the centre of the early Pentecostal movement. The first, unsurprisingly, is the re-emergence of spiritual gifts – speaking in tongues, prophecy and especially healing. For 1500 years or more, it had been assumed that these gifts had been reserved for the apostolic or pre-Constantinian period of the church. It was precisely the fundamentalists and theologians of Reformed Orthodoxy who put up the fiercest resistance to the Pentecostals, holding on to "Cessationism" – the idea that all miraculous spiritual gifts in the church had ceased and would not return again. The burden of proof was on the Pentecostals: they had to show that their gifts were authentic – and at the same time explain why they had reappeared after such a long time. The historical gap between the Early Church and the church of the present even made the authenticity of the gifts seriously questionable.

The historical explanation was found by joining forces with the growing missionary movement. This is the second reason why eschatology is pivotal in the early Pentecostal movement. Protestants were increasingly sceptical towards mission. Some were even of the opinion that mission in foreign lands was also a feature of the apostolic age, like spiritual gifts, and had no validity in their own time and place. Nevertheless, at the beginning of the 18th century, some Lutherans and other Protestants began to devote themselves seriously to mission. Later, in the 19th century, foreign missions were so important to the identity of Protestant churches – and ultimately to the structure of Christianity around the world! – that they became a central feature of ecclesiology and of reflection on church history.

So what the earliest Pentecostals did was to make a connection between their spectacular new spiritual gifts and mission, linking them both with the end times, based on Mark 13:10: "And the good news must first be proclaimed to all nations." Here the key to the delay of Christ's return could be found: not all nations had heard the Gospel yet! And what was the greatest obstacle to hearing the Gospel? Literally the language barrier! This is how Charles Fox Parham, at whose school William J. Seymour studied, explained the gift of tongues: he understood it as xenolalia, the unmediated communication with foreigners, and not as → glossolalia, the language of the angels.

While there are occasional and isolated reports of sudden, miraculous speaking in foreign languages, it seems that no missionary was ever given the complete and lifelong gift of fluency in a foreign language without study. But this did not deter the Pentecostals from their enthusiasm for missions and spiritual gifts. The more important realisation was that Christ could not return until "his" Christians had fulfilled their task of sharing the gospel with the whole world. But when they had done so, Christ would certainly return. This gave a strong sense of urgency to the work of global missions. There is no denying that Pentecostals displayed a level of energy and commitment to world missions that is unparalleled in the whole of church history.

Of course, no movement or theology in the church remains static; it evolves over time. For some Pentecostals, charismatics and neo-charismatics, the idea that Christ could return at any time remains central to their preaching. Others, meanwhile, have quietly put aside their eschatological expectations of a Second Coming in the near future and instead, like all Christian movements before them, have invested in the long term by setting up institutions. The founding of a Pentecostal church or university is no longer a contradiction in terms.

Within the Pentecostal spectrum, some have turned to premillenarianism, best expressed by John Nelson Darby, the father of the Plymouth Brethren and the Scofield Study Bible. The popular series of "Left Behind" novels shows a strong commitment to "deciphering" the book of Revelation in order to get a road map of the end times and bring Christians onto the right side of history. Further variants of Pentecostalism pursue one recent manifestation of the Spirit or the other and dismiss other churches, movements or stages of Pentecostalism as "backwards".

In their confessions, the historical Protestant churches hold to the view that it is not permitted to predict exact dates for the end of time. The Augsburg Confession of 1530 rejects teachings "which teach that, before the resurrection of the dead, saints and godly men will possess a worldly kingdom and annihilate all the godless" (CA 17). In the same speech in which Jesus says that the gospel must first be preached to all nations, he says: "But about that day or hour no one knows, neither the angels in heaven, nor the Son, but only the Father" (Mk 13:32). Attempts to frighten believers or to over-interpret current events should be rejected immediately.

On the other hand, this does not justify complacency or indifference on the part of the churches. It is no coincidence that the Pentecostal hope in the "Soon Coming King" triggered an impassioned worldwide missionary movement. It is remarkable that parallel to the explosive growth of Pentecostalism in the 20th century, biblical scholarship has also rediscovered the importance of the apocalyptic for the New Testament. It may be wrong to determine the end all too precisely, but it would be just as wrong to forget the end altogether. A healthy church will certainly plant its little apple trees for tomorrow – but it should be ready every day to be called to account for the state of its orchard.

3.7 What threatens us: Spirits and demons

Apart from eschatology, it is the Pentecostal concept of evil spirits and demons that often seems strange. As a rule, it comes in connection with simple allusion to the devil or Satan as a person, whereby it is doubtful whether that is meant metaphorically or it is believed to be real. German Pentecostal congregations often strongly reject the "belief in demons" and interpret it as part of a non-European, "pre-Christian" culture. Belief in demons is indeed particularly prevalent in Pentecostal churches with a West African cultural background. This applies to Pentecostal churches in West Africa as well as to congregations familiar to us with a West African background; but it is also true, for example, for Brazilian Pentecostal churches with their strong need to be distinguished from those Afro-Brazilian cults which are also influenced by West African religious and cultural traditions and their belief in demons. These churches would for their part vehemently reject the assumption that they have taken over these forms of piety from African tribal religions. They would rather draw attention to biblical texts that mention Satan or report how Jesus himself exorcised demons. However, there is a widespread idea that the spirits worshipped in some African religions do not only exist, but are actually demons that need to be cast out.

It is possible, however, that in our German (post-modern?) culture the confusion with regard to demons is also dwindling. As mentioned above in chapter 3.5, this topic is familiar in highbrow entertainment literature, films and musicals ("The Lord of the Rings", "Harry Potter", "Buffy the Vampire Slayer") and in computer games. Have we not long since become accustomed to "beaming" ourselves into another reality for the sake of entertainment, without even thinking about its nature in real life?

Not to mention shamanistic and other healing rituals that are supposed to liberate one from demonic possession and are now booming, not just at esoteric fairs.

Pentecostal piety, in any case, exerts a considerable part of its fascination by giving room to experiences of overcoming evil. Among Pentecostals these experiences can be seen in beliefs such as "*spiritual warfare*", exorcist methods for driving out "evil spirits" or general empowerment to deal with evil, which is sometimes imagined in a very tangible form. Religious sociology interprets this as religious compensation for the fact that Pentecostal believers are socially underprivileged. However, these practices are such an integral part of Pentecostal Christianity in various regions of the world that this cannot be the only explanation. At the same time, it is noteworthy that corresponding expressions of the Christian faith are not completely unknown in traditional denominational churches – even if they have meanwhile become very rare in most cases. Two examples might be named. The Catholic Church still allows exorcist rituals under narrowly defined conditions. And during the last major reform of the baptismal order of service in German Protestantism (2000), the Evangelical Church of the Union re-introduced liturgical denials of evil and the devil (the so-called *abrenuntiatio diaboli*) as a special option in adult baptism. It is interesting that the latter happened although such formulas had not been practised for decades. For large parts of the Early Church, the reality of evil was perfectly normal, both physically and in the flesh, and even the reformer Luther spoke frequently and gladly of "sin, death and the devil" in one breath. Centuries ago, theologians built up complicated doctrinal structures concerning so-called demonology, dealing with the powers of evil in contrast to the doctrine of angels (angelology).

These meager remnants of the theme of overcoming evil in the traditional confessional churches admittedly do not compare to the prominence of this subject in Pentecostalism. Accordingly, there is very little basis on which both sides could reach agreement, for example, if one refers to the New Testament claim that being a Christian includes the ability to "test the spirits" (1 John 4:1 ff.) and thus to master those ("evil") spirits that do not agree with God's Spirit. This observation calls for an explanation, but also makes the topic intellectually appealing and could lead to increased interest in a well-moderated congregational discussion.

Theologically, the prevailing doctrinal view in the traditional denominational churches tends to refer indirectly to the disempowerment of evil in the context of salvation and the forgiveness of sins. A classic example is the insight of the Church Father Augustine (354–430), gained in the course of a lifelong, literally biographical struggle. Before his baptism in 396, he was long inclined towards the harshly dualistic religion of Manichaeism, until he came to the realisation that evil cannot be a power on a par with God. For that would negate God's uniqueness and love. One can say Christianity basically believes that God will ultimately persevere in the face of evil, even if he now still has to fight against the anti-divine. The so-called principal dualism does not assume that there is an imbalance between God and evil, but both are seen as at least equally strong. An evil anti-principle or an anti-God stands in opposition to and on an equal footing with the Creator. This view has been regarded since the Middle Ages as a characteristic of sectarian or heretical groups. In the modern age, the Swiss reformer Karl Barth (1886–1968) formulated the same idea, adopting lines of thought from the medieval Jewish reform theologian Moses

Maimonides (circa 1135–1204). This concept accords no independent reality to evil; it exists at best as "nothingness" of an abstract nature. Just as every "yes" is based on an implicit "no", on something that the "yes" denies, so is God's love an implicit combat against the anti-divine – loving it away, as it were. Nevertheless, evil still continues to work in this world a practical problem that could also, or even particularly, be discussed with Pentecostal congregations, for whom this is also a reality. In any event, the question of evil maintains its position alongside all faith in salvation solely on the basis of the life experience of every human being. Pentecostal piety, which speaks of evil in a personalised way, as a reality in the form of a person or a (good or evil) spirit in a house or other place (so-called *territorial spirits*), correlates to this experience very closely. The personalisation of the experience of evil finds its expression in language, at least. Is it even possible that it is easier to cope with the concrete threat of evil to one's own person if it comes in a personal form, so that one can identify a concrete culprit who is responsible for the effects of evil? Maybe the traditional confessional churches are not quite unfamiliar with this view: after all, the seventh petition of the Lord's Prayer speaks of deliverance from "evil". The definite article to be found here in the German text of the Lord's Prayer – "the evil" – can be both neuter and masculine, as it is in the original Greek New Testament. Without recourse to any mythical notion of devils and anti-gods, this can mean not only "what" is evil, but also "who" is evil. This simple linguistic observation on one of the texts which are indisputably fundamental to Christianity may perhaps direct our attention to some theological traditions that raise less dogmatic and more practical aspects on the problem of evil, namely a) prayer, b) the Christian worldview and c) the Christian virtues.

a) Prayer

The ambiguity of the seventh petition of the Lord's Prayer reminds us that all the petitions of this exemplary *prayer* have a double meaning. On the one hand, their subject is the specific need of those praying; on the other, they regularly touch on a meaning which goes beyond the specific. One example is the daily bread which is also a symbol of the "great banquet", an image of the Kingdom of God in the New Testament Gospels. Thus, deliverance from evil also aims not only at the avoidance of a reduction of life, but also at the achievement of eternal life, life which is in itself good and no longer threatened by any powers of evil. When Pentecostal Christians speak of evil as a person whom they conquer through their faith, that can be a reminder that the prayer for the coming of the Kingdom of God is spoken in the whole of Christianity.

b) The Christian worldview

The remarks above may also explain the relationship with an apocalyptic *worldview*, which often embraces the Pentecostal expectation of the overcoming of evil (see above chap. 3.6). The victory of good over evil is here seen in connection with a final battle involving upheavals of cosmic proportions. This can apparently be brought into line with a religious interpretation of all kinds of phenomena from global history, politics or science, whether it be world wars or the mortality of bees. Such opinions found in the apocalyptic worldview are often met with widespread scepticism in wider Christian circles and are regarded as dualistic fixations. In its literal sense, however, the apocalyptic worldview refers to the unveiling (Greek *apokálypsis*) of the future. It therefore does not automatically entail the principle of dualism that the classical churches from Augustine to Barth ruled out for Christianity. The apocalyptic worldview emphasises the future orientation of the divine creator's power, which will also prevail over crises and threats which may still be unimaginable today ("new creation"). In this sense, apocalypticism is currently being rediscovered as a radical new creation in both Protestant and Roman Catholic theology – another possible bridge to the conversation with Pentecostal churches.

c) The Christian virtues

The reference to God's creative love further evokes the theme complex of the Christian *virtues*, which include faith and hope alongside love. The link between them is the subject of the Christian doctrine of providence, which also offers an effective theological approach to the problem of evil, for it considers the way in which God's work of salvation is reflected in the concrete life of an individual and the community. Real life is seen to mirror the comprehensive divine work of salvation. Applied to the problem of evil, this means that hope in God's final overcoming of evil is reflected in the patience of individuals who withstand the reality of evil in their lives. Both hope and patience are virtues in dealing with suffering or want, which they counter with God's reality. Hope takes refuge in this reality, thus looking beyond present afflictions, while patience enables people to persevere in the present time. People who demonstrate patience are made free and open to new and different ways in which God's reality enters their lives – ways other than those people hope for in their prayers, possibly. In the language of Pentecostals, this is a process of "empowerment". The relationship between hope and patience is at the same time characteristic for the Christian belief in prov-idence, because it assumes that God has as many solutions as there are people who hope in him. The certainty that the power of Jesus will and must overcome real-life evil can be observed over and over again in Pentecostal churches, and it is understandable against the background of the doctrine of providence developed in the traditional confessional church-es. Similarly, the virtue of patience in dealing with the prob-lem of evil forms a bridge between the theology of the clas-sical Christian churches and the Pentecostal expectation of "empowerment".

3.8 How we experience salvation: Prayer, healing, blessing, empowerment

Greek Orthodox believers who go to church on the day of Epi-phany (6 January) take home some water that has been blessed during the service. It is a visible sign of blessing for the whole of the following year and is carefully kept at home. If some-one from family or friends falls ill, they apply or drink a little of this water. Theologically, this is not interpreted as the ad-ministration of a magic potion, but as a spiritual reaffirmation of baptism – an act of remembrance and renewal. This, in turn, serves to strengthen the certainty of God's presence, founded in baptism. Orthodox theology also refers to this as the presence of divine energies in the lives of the believers.[22]

---

22 *Athanasios Vletsis*, Sakramente als Ort der Begegnung der gesamten Schöpfung mit dem Drei-einigen Gott, in: *Ulrike Link-Wieczorek/Uwe Swarat* (eds.), Die Frage nach Gott heute. Ökume-nische Impulse zum Gespräch mit dem „Neuen Atheismus" (BÖR 111), Leipzig 2017, 290–301, esp. 291.

⊙ Case study: Living Faith Ministry, Bremen

There are still a few old buildings in Walle, a district in the west of Bremen, but it consists mostly of terraced houses and apartment blocks from the 1950 s and 1960 s as well as large warehouses in its docklands and also Bremen's ambitious urban development scheme "Überseestadt". The district was almost totally destroyed in 1945 and is today gaining a specific, increasingly intercultural flair. This is the home of the young Afro-Pentecostal congregation "Living Faith Ministry". It takes a moment to find it at the address given after leaving the tram that runs through the busy Heerstrasse in Walle. The church premises are in a warehouse at the end of a car park. But when you get inside and go into the church, the functional industrial atmosphere turns into a different world: soft plush carpeting, rows of chairs with red velvet upholstery and brass-coloured legs, undecorated white walls and a huge cross on the front wall behind a stage with band equipment: drums, amplifier, keyboard, microphone. Before these instruments literally come into play, there is a Bible study. Four of the seat rows are filled. A teacher tells a story of how Jesus cast out demons; the listeners attempt to describe in various ways how demons work in our modern world. They seduce people to live a "bad life", to take drugs and drink and behave badly. Gradually, the remaining rows of chairs fill up. Families with younger children stay at the back. The members of the band take their seats, three women in white dresses lead the singing of the congregation with rich and powerful voices. People come forward to dance together, first the men, then the women. After an hour of praise, the service itself begins with prayers, singing and a sermon by Pastor Stephen Achiriki which becomes more and more emotional. He tells of the death of a 15-year-old girl who was seriously ill; her father had called him to pray at her bedside, but after four days and four nights the girl died, as the doctors had already predicted. The congregation is deeply moved and accompanies the story with exclamations and loud sighs. What now? Is this a story of Pentecostal failure? The end of the sermon brings a well of hope. After the girl's funeral, her grandmother, who had travelled from Romania and was at her bedside as the people prayed for her, joined the church as a new member. Obviously, it is not the direct fulfilment of prayer requests that makes the comfort and help of the Holy Spirit perceptible. A similar effect can be seen when the "devils are driven out" of people who are sick or disabled, who publicly reveal themselves as such during the service and come forward to the pastor, so that he may ask them to be released from the hold of the demons. This is done with a loud voice and strong gestures. The people go back to their places, limping and coughing. By this time at the latest, the entire congregation knows of their troubles. By going public, do they find increased hope of recognition and solidarity? We do not know exactly how God answers our prayers, said some young people in a discussion group with Protestant students from Oldenburg, but there is no doubt that the Holy Spirit gives us strength through them. The small Pentecostal congregation consists of about 70 congregants, the majority of which are African migrants. But there are also people from a Latin American context and a young (Catholic) woman from Bremen with no migration background as well as a family from Oldenburg. The common language is English, but the pastor's daughter, a student, translates the entire service into German if necessary. The pastor sees the speaking in tongues as an opportunity to "give God more time" and to feel his influence. A "fall-down-culture", in which participants at the service fall to the ground in ecstasy, is not cultivated in the Bremen congregation, even though it can happen. In the case that it does the member of the congregation has to explain to the pastor what exactly changes in his life afterwards.

The congregation is an institutionally independent offshoot of the Hamburg "Christ Church Outreach Mission". Pastor Achiriki and his wife come from Ghana and speak some of the African languages of that country as well as that of the Yoruba. Their parents belonged to an African tribal religion – "idol worshippers", as Achiriki says. He himself became a Pentecostal Christian through evangelisation in Ghana. The story of a pickpocket who found Christ and changed his life convinced him. Later, in Hamburg, he attended the Pentecostal "Laymen Bible School" for three years. Today, the trained mechanical engineer works in Bremen and is in charge of the congregation on a voluntary basis. At present, he and ten members of the congregation are attending a three-year theology course run by the Association of Pentecostal Churches in Erzhausen.

Three years ago, the Bremen "Living Faith Ministry" congregation took part with great enthusiasm in the "Ecumenical Hospitality Relay", in which various Bremen churches invited each other for a visit. However, there has still not been any exchange of theological opinions, which Achiriki regrets. "They prefer to come and see us dance," he says, commenting on these experiences – maybe a reflection of intercultural stereotypes?

Every year, a large number of Roman Catholics from all over the world (estimates run into the millions) travel to the Grotto of Massabielle in the small town of Lourdes in south-western France – mostly in organised parish groups – to pray for the healing of illnesses or disabilities and to drink or bathe in the healing waters of the spring that bubbles up here. The pilgrimage site is dedicated to the Virgin Mary, who is said to have appeared to a young local girl here in 1858. Some of the visitors come regularly. Despite the fact that they and many others leave with the same handicap they came with, they feel strengthened by the pilgrimage.

In a small Pentecostal congregation in Bremen, whose members mainly come from an African background, people acknowledge their illnesses at a certain point during the Sunday service. They come forward to the pastor so that he can loudly cast out the demons responsible for their condition.

Since around the turn of the millennium, rituals for the anointing of the sick or regular "anointing services" have been introduced in a number of Protestant regional churches and have found a place in the service orders of the VELKD (United Evangelical Lutheran Church of Germany). The Rhenish Church understands them as a sign of a holistic perception of human life as creaturely life.

When Pentecostal churches associate the presence of the Holy Spirit with healing, praying for it and invoking a blessing, this is in no way a strange concept for Christianity. Admittedly, the Reformation broke away from a broader understanding of the sacraments, such as is still practised today in the Orthodox and Catholic traditions, and concentrated on the general promise of the "word" preached. This probably helped to avoid a "magical misunderstanding" of a more sensual symbolism. However, we can observe, not least in recent developments in pastoral care, that the Protestant churches are also in search of a more sensory, holistic and tangible liturgical representation of God's loving care. In this context, Pentecostal piety contributes to the ecumenical dialogue and the search for expressions of faith. The question will be how the credo of God's freedom can be preserved.

The Pentecostal-charismatic movements emphasise the close connection between healing and salvation or redemption. They also place enthusiastic and emotional experiences at the centre of their piety, interpreting them as manifestations of the Holy Spirit. However, they also emphasise the comforting, even *power-giving* effect of the Spirit, which is called "empowerment". The believers feel strengthened in their everyday life to rely on their chances for (self-)development even in difficult life situations. Within the Pentecostal-charismatic spectrum believers experience salvation in various forms and interpretations. In the next sections, Pentecostal concepts and practices of prayer, healing and blessing will be reflected upon and the general concept of empowerment will be presented.

a) Prayer

Prayer forms the basis of Pentecostal-charismatic worship services, with the specific emphasis on pneumatic praise and thanksgiving. This form of prayer is particularly accompanied by music. Before the actual service, the visitors spend a lot of time in praise; they do not arrive at church at a certain time and the service does not start punctually. The "songs of praise" are accompanied or literally "gets things going" by a band, drums, guitar, keyboard and other instruments, as well as by singers leading the worship, whose voices are often impressive (see below chapter 3.9). These prayers of thanksgiving have a completely different ring to those of classical services. It is as if the practical relationship with God is explicitly exercised in the atmosphere of profane joy. This is also reflected in the architecture of the churches and church halls, which resemble venues for pop concerts rather than traditional places of worship. This is no coincidence.

It is also striking that there is hardly any room for lamentation during the prayers in the services. Confession of sin and lamentation over past suffering are virtually drowned out by the atmosphere of praise, it seems. Nonetheless, there is an indirect reference to these themes, especially when the praise is replaced by intercession. When prayers are offered for healing or the driving out of some evil power (see chapter 3.7), then there is certainly a sense of the adversities of life, but this takes place within the strongly emphasised hope for change through the presence of the Spirit. How this will happen is not usually explained in detail, so that the realisation is placed in the hands of God. A particularly powerful and authoritative prayer (usually by the pastor) is staged in such a way that it indeed seems to give rise to emotional hope for a causal effect. This is strengthened by the fact that it is a typos of Pentecostal evangelisation to tell stories of healing done by casting out → demons. The spectator at such performances can gain the impression that it is no longer assumed that God is inaccessible. This kind of demonological interpretation can lead to a dualistic world view. But they can also become an expression of contextual tensions in the lives of those praying for God's help. Basically, these practices also pose the question to the traditional confessional churches as to how they would describe their understanding of absolution. This could be a subject of discussion in conversations with Pentecostal congregations about belief.

In most Pentecostal congregations in Germany, praying in "tongues" in a non-existent language (→ glossolalia), is no longer considered a necessary condition and indispensable sign of a genuine experience of the Spirit. Where it does take place, it is often seen by the worshippers to be a sign of intense devotion in prayer.

The tendencies influenced by the Pentecostal Word of Faith movement assume that the Spirit is the all-determining reality of humans. Following Romans 10:9, the idea is that reality is created by the imaginative power of the Spirit, by confession of the lips and the proclamation of divine power. The prayer for redemption through the presence of God in his Spirit is often formulated as a request for health, wealth, and material prosperity. Here one must ask how far some Pentecostal congregations even attribute reality-changing power to this supplication – in a very concrete sense. A faith dialogue with Pentecostal congregations could also cover the concept of supplication; members of traditional denominational congregations would be challenged to explain how they understand this kind of prayer.

Pentecostal piety thus encourages us to rethink forms of prayer in the historical Protestant churches as well. Since the Reformation (with the individualisation and subjectivisation of faith), prayer has mainly been understood as a dialogue of the human heart with God, in thanksgiving, praise and requests for forgiveness, help, strength and comfort. There are different forms of prayer, both alone and in groups. Should we find it difficult to find words, pre-formulated prayers such as the Lord's Prayer, the Psalms and other prayer texts are helpful. Prayer as intercession trusts in God's saving will and submits to it. It takes place in the certain knowledge that God hears our prayers.

The person praying should not force God to fulfil wishes, but trust that the answer to prayer can also happen in a way other than asked. Such practices, which are very much focused on the inwardness of religion, are a phenomenon of the modern age. Apart from these, there have always been forms of piety that were oriented towards the transformation of dire situations.

b) Healing

The Pentecostal expectation of *healing* through the Spirit can be described as a special form of prayer experience. It is of central significance in Pentecostal-charismatic movements. Healing the sick is considered a spiritual gift. Similar to the prayer for healing at the sick bed in the pastoral care of confessional churches, the Pentecostal prayer for healing is not necessarily understood as a substitute for medical treatment. But empirically experienced "successes" of Pentecostal healing practices are pointed out, for example in reports on evangelisations or in testimonies at services. The Pentecostal prayer for healing is a request for the (spontaneous) healing of a sick person by the Holy Spirit, supported by the laying on of hands, by contact and anointing. The guiding theological idea is that the Spirit can overcome limitations and work in a surprising way, fulfilling the work of *Christus praesens* (see chapter 3.5 on Christology). There is a noticeably close connection between the healing ministry and the prayer for deliverance from demonic powers, which are literally addressed as the cause of numerous illnesses, compulsions and disorders.

All Christians are called upon to pray for healing. This raises awareness for a dimension that has been forgotten and neglected in the churches of the Reformation. At the same time, Pentecostal churches connect with the yearning for healing that people already had at the time of Jesus, in the Early Church and up to the present day, and which leads them to ask questions about God. The belief in demons, which in Pentecostal churches goes back not least to non-European influences and in this respect originates from a specific cultural "language stream", proves to be a topic that needs to be reconsidered from a theological and cultural point of view (see chapter 3.7). However, it should not be overlooked that practices of exorcisms are also known in Western Christianity, e. g. in the Roman Catholic Church.

In principle, it must be emphasised that faith which trusts in the healing power of God does not contradict the use of specialist medical help. By referring back to Jesus Christ, the healer, this is being rediscovered in theology and the church. The fact that new charismatic congregations insist on rejecting the enlightened worldview has to be seen in a critical and self-critical light.

The Pentecostal understanding of healing, which emphasises the optimistic hope of cure, is possibly a question for Christendom as a whole. Where should we draw a line under excessive promises of healing, and what role is played here by the experience of the problem of theodicy? Does the Christian faith not also include the dark side of Christian spirituality, such as experiences of gloom, hardship and forsakenness? All in all, the limitations and brokenness of human life should not be ignored. Can believers not experience God's healing nearness, even if they are not healed in body or soul? Naturally, these questions can also throw us back to the reality of the mainstream churches: do they not drown out the biblical view, which clearly voices suffering, with banal and commonplace phrases? Do we not also need clearer forms of lament, of calling from the depths and of asking for God's presence in such real-life situations?

There is no doubt, however, that Pentecostal healing practices, with all their confidence in being saved, must also be understood as an eschatological thematisation of the darker aspects of life, as a method to overcome them. It is even possible that in the practice of fervent healing prayer the reassurance of the community of believers plays a greater role than the concrete fulfilment of prayer. This question arises not least in view of the ecumenical breadth of related practices alluded to at the beginning.

c) Blessing

The *blessing* is another form of the promise of salvation. It corresponds particularly well to the concerns of Pentecostal theology in so far as, in the biblical view, God's work of blessing aims to give concrete success in life to individuals and their surroundings, including the material resources required. In church services, spiritual counselling or everyday rituals, God's blessing is granted on his behalf, as it were, to someone else in the grammatical form of a wish – basically a reassurance that God's actions have the fundamental character of a blessing on each specific life. At the same time, the person receiving the blessing passes it on as a witness to the ongoing effect of God's blessing for the benefit of others – "You shall be a blessing". This liturgical practice, which is common to other denominational traditions, has mainly come to be seen as a Pentecostal speciality as a result of the "Toronto Blessing" in 1994. Here, the blessing with the Holy Spirit led to certain extraordinary and spectacular manifestations of the presence of the Spirit among the blessed. All over the world, uncontrolled laughing, weeping, trembling and falling was widespread in Pentecostal services, marking the so-called Third Wave of Pentecostal-charismatic Christianity. In these groups, blessing, laying on of hands and anointing are of particular importance. For example, they can see the laying on of hands during the blessing as a rediscovery of biblical aspects (e.g. Heb 6:2) and as a response to the need for bodily contact. It helps believers to experience God's love physically.

Pentecostal-charismatic Christianity has drawn renewed attention to biblical themes that had been neglected in Protestant Christianity, such as the laying on of hands, blessing and anointing. Pentecostal and churches of other denominations can jointly consider whether the request for and the promise of God's blessing can be understood as a means of causally bringing about the effect of blessing. There is criticism of Pentecostals and a certain form of charismatic piety because they risk a restriction in their understanding of blessing: it then seems that good health, prosperity and success are the direct effects of strong faith and a Christian way of life. On the contrary, illness, poverty and failure cannot lead to the conclusion that a person's faith is too small and their conduct of life unchristian. Ultimately, it is God's presence which is blessing, sustaining all that promotes life. Blessing cannot be compelled or forcibly connected with expectations of good fortune. Such problems were certainly discussed in the past by traditional theologies, e.g. the Calvinist doctrine of predestination. Here, too, it was pointed out that it would be a misunderstanding to regard wealth and prosperity as the primary and sole measure of blessing.

d) Empowerment

One basic characteristic giving Pentecostals a feeling of certainty of the healing presence of the Spirit is the experience of *empowerment,* which arises through prayer, healing, blessing, but also fellowship. Empowerment is a term which is well-known in liberation theology and pedagogy, but also in the context of social work. It concerns possibilities of changing one's own life situation and behaviour in order to improve one's living conditions, i.e. a resource-oriented approach. Instead of focusing on the deficits, whether personal, financial or social, the aim is directed towards the (self-)creative possibilities. For many members of Pentecostal churches in the Global South (but also in migrant churches in Germany), life has been marked by deprivation: many have little access to formal education, an unstable economic situation, and hardly any opportunity to participate satisfactorily in social affairs. They are marginalised and have often internalised this sense of marginalisation in feelings of shame and guilt.

In this context, the experience of being directly filled with God's Spirit is often felt so drastically that it leads to a permanent change in life. Despite failing education, financial need, and low social status, believers may assume that they have access, in an egalitarian way, to a source of power and strength that is greater than all the insurmountable barriers that have previously blocked their chances in life. At the same time, they experience the fellowship in which they are integrated as a second home, a place where they belong in spite of migration and mobility. An intensive, mostly also digitally supported network of relationships, where they pray for and help one another, enables them to establish bonds similar to those of a family.

The experience of empowerment is therefore extremely holistic: it fulfils spiritual and psychosocial needs in equal measure, supports the need to find healing, meaning and identity in the midst of brokenness and flaws and to be liberated from unwholesome bonds of the past. Often it is the immediate physical and emotional closeness to Jesus – in forms of ecstasy – that provides emotional security, self-respect and practical orientation in life, the beginning of a positive change for the future.

Such changes through empowerment are visible both individually and socially. For many people, it provides an impetus to develop their own initiative and capability for action, often manifested in the assumption of personal responsibility in church, family and profession. Studies on the connection between Pentecostalism, family ethics and economic activity in different contexts confirm this development. They show that strategies of developmental policy aimed at the political and economic empowerment of marginalised people must be preceded by their subjective experience of personal, meaningful empowerment. Only then do people perceive themselves as empowered and strengthened, so that they can personally understand, interpret and take an active part in changing their way of life economically and socially.

However, when Pentecostal congregations are in search of profound empowerment experiences, they can slip into the abuse of power and the establishment of rigid hierarchies. In many megachurches, for example, the founders and charismatic leaders, or even Pentecostal missionaries such as Reinhard Bonnke (⊙ "Christ for all Nations"), sometimes stage themselves as "powerful men of God" and are revered as such. They ostensibly have constant access to divine authority, which they activate in order to drive out evil spirits and enable believers to lead a successful life in every respect. In this way, they resemble the figure of Jesus in the Synoptic Gospels more closely than the apostles in Acts, for the former has permanent authority and miraculous power, while the latter appear as petitioners and mediators of numinous power, continuously dependent on the exalted Christ.

Bible texts on *exousia* (Greek for authority, power, command) are suitable when speaking with members of Pentecostal churches on the topic of empowerment. There is a fundamental conviction in Pentecostal Christianity that believers share in the Holy Spirit and that they can be empowered by the presence of the Holy Spirit to perform extraordinary spiritual deeds. The prerequisite for this is the baptism of faith and a subsequent experience of being baptised by and with the Holy Spirit. To support this conviction, Pentecostals refer above all to some passages in the Acts of the Apostles. However, it is not possible to verify such a uniform conception biblically, neither within the New Testament nor in Acts. The notion that believers are generally endowed with *exousia* is also not to be found in New Testament texts. Rather, the synoptic texts speak of Jesus endowing his narrowly defined circle of disciples with the authority to cast out demons or unclean spirits.[23]

The leading question in such a discussion could concern the specific understanding of *exousia:* what experiences are linked to the idea of empowerment as a resource for setting in motion processes of change in oneself and others to promote reconciliation and liberation? What form does this power take? Is there a difference between human power and divine power? What can be said about the inaccessibility of empowerment and the suffering of the righteous? And how can the very real experiences of helplessness and limitation correspond to experiences of empowerment?

---

23 Cf. Mt 10:1; Mk 6:7; Lk 9:1 etc.; cf. also Acts 1:8: endowment of the apostles by the Holy Spirit with *dynamis*: miraculous power.

⊙ **Case study: Yoido Full Gospel Church**

The Yoido Full Gospel Church in Seoul, South Korea, is one of the world's largest → megachurches. For a long time, it consisted of a single congregation on Yoi Island in the South Korean capital. Several thousand people come here several times a day to pray and worship. The main auditorium seats 10,000 visitors, and the events there are transmitted into several smaller halls. Modern translation technology allows people of different nations and languages to follow the services. The first service on Yoi Island was held in 1973. Since then, the congregation has grown to over 800,000 members, so that satellite congregations have been founded that are closely linked to the mother church. The Yoido Full Gospel Church is considered the largest congregation in the world.

Closely associated with the Yoido Full Gospel Church is the name of the founder David Yonggi Cho (born in 1936); he has since handed over his position to his successor Young Hoon Lee. As in many Pentecostal megachurches, the story of how the church was founded and the biography of the founding father play a major role. In 1958, after his theology studies, Cho began to hold the first services with five people in the flat of a friend who later became his mother-in-law. He himself tells how they later had to move the growing group to hold their services in a tent. In the 1960s, the group experienced enormous growth and was soon able to purchase a plot of land and build a meeting place for 1,000 people there.

Unlike many other successful charismatic megachurches, the Yoido Full Gospel Church has not refused to speak with other Christian churches and traditions. It was in close contact with the World Council of Churches before and during its 10th Assembly in Busan in 2013. Pastor Lee was vice-chairperson of the Korean Host Committee for the Assembly. The Yoido Full Gospel Church has formulated a theology that has been heavily criticised by theologians of the historical Protestant tradition, but has always been open to dialogue. David Yonggi Cho himself sought dialogue with Jürgen Moltmann, although the latter was close to the politically oriented Korean liberation theology, the so-called Minjung theology of the 1980s. Cho sent theologians all over the world to study theology and to do doctorates and did not reject contact with academic theology – as many other Pentecostal church leaders do.

The theology of Yoido Full Gospel Church is often reduced to one simple formula, the doctrine of the Three-Fold Blessing and the Four-Fold Gospel. The doctrine of the Four-Fold Gospel is the original theological approach formulated by Albert Benjamin Simpson at the end of the 19th century and found in various versions in Pentecostal circles. It describes the four-fold identity, significance and role of Jesus as Saviour, Saint, Healer and Son of God. This is expressed in the gospel of *regeneration*, *holiness*, *divine healing* and the Second Coming of the Lord (*advent*).

The Three-Fold Blessing (blessing of the spirit, soul and body) is based on this Christological pattern. The fact that blessings play such an important role, and that the members expect tangible material and health benefits from their participation in prayers and services, locates the Yoido Full Gospel Church among the churches that preach a → *prosperity gospel*. Here, too, the motto is: to those who give much, much will be given. Money plays a big role during the services, being collected in hundreds of velvety red collection bags and piled up on a specially prepared table. It gives an impressive picture of the congregation's affluence and the blessing shared by all those who make it possible to collect such abundance.

However, in the meantime, the Yoido Full Gospel Church has also suffered the fate of Korea's massive secularisation. Growth has come to a standstill. And with that, the congregation has lost its unique selling point of a faith community that miraculously and permanently multiplies itself. The growth itself was already the content of the message: we are many and are becoming more and more. We are convincing, we are successful, with us you are on the winning track and upward bound. David Yonggi Cho drives luxury limousines and has cult status, which was not even diminished by his conviction in 2014 for irregularities in the handling of church finances. It will be interesting to see how this congregation will fare in times of secularisation.

3.9 What makes us sing: Music and spirituality

In most religions, music is used specifically to praise God, to create communion and to give ritual acts a dramatic form. Music also plays an essential role in the Judeo-Christian context. Its main task is doxological and at the same time pastoral: to bring God praises or lamentations and thus also to bring balm to the soul. This already took place in the Psalter of biblical times with sounds and songs; the temple cult in Jerusalem employed many musicians for this purpose. It is possible to distinguish between various basic aspects of musical practice with differing degrees of anthropological and theological emphasis: the (psycho-)somatic "biogenic" aspects of music and singing, which have an effect on the body, bring rhythm, melody, harmony and sound design into close connection with emotional bodily processes. Music stimulates movement, thereby homogenising cultic communities and enabling dramaturgical control of moods and atmospheres. It energises and offers psychological *empowerment* and strong *involvement* as people sing and make music together. Looking back to ancient Greek cults with ecstatic music and being aware of the manipulative possibilities of music in creating a mood, theology has been critical of music throughout history, ranging from Augustine through Zwingli to (moderate) Calvin, down to the modern-day music theology of Joseph Ratzinger (which harmonises with evangelical warnings on pop and rock music). Following this criticism, the mainstream of European church music has focused more on the "logogenic" aspect of music, seeing it as an artistic form of audible communication which can deepen language and thus make interpretation easier. (In addition, however, more somatically oriented forms of subcultural popular piety also survived). Typologically, one could also trace these two aspects back to the Pauline debate on the right use of → glossolalia and the plea for proclamation in a rational, intelligible language.

Charismatic and Pentecostal churches now focus primarily on the biogenic ecstatic/glossolalic/somatic dimension of musical performance. On the surface level, texts do play a certain role, concentrating on the strongly Bible-centred theological convictions of these congregations (biblical statements about God and the emphasis on his grace are popular, but most of the songs praise the name of Jesus and his kingship). However, it would be a misunderstanding of the heart of this phenomenon, were one to focus primarily on the lyrics of these songs in a hermeneutic-critical approach, for example by criticising the thoughtless patriarchal language. It is the sounds and rhythms which are important, intended as they are to conjure up and sustain a particular, elated mood. The idea is to stimulate integration into the collective fellowship of worshippers, to create a "holy" atmosphere and transform emotions (which can also culminate in conversions). This praise music is currently so successful for two reasons: on the one hand, it ties in with the tradition of pietistic hymns, which combine the fostering of personal, heartfelt piety with an emotionally direct, doxological devotion to Jesus and a strong orientation to fellowship. In the late modern age with its individualisation and pluralisation of cultural patterns, this offers an attractive religious experience without bewildering complexity. At the same time, by radically adapting to the methods of production, distribution and reception in mainstream pop music, it overcomes the disturbing gulf to the leading present-day pop culture.

The roots of this music genre lie in the charismatic renewal movement of the 1960s in Anglican, Presbyterian and Lutheran churches in the USA, which also spread to the Catholic Church at the end of the decade. The second half of the 1970s saw the founding of the *Vineyard* movement in southern California, which organised praise worship services with music in the style of folk rock and other genres. In the context of the Jesus Movement in California, a series of records entitled *Praise* was produced from 1972 onwards, which also attracted attention in Germany. From the 1980s onwards, and especially in the 1990s, lavishly arranged praise and worship songs, often modelled on American pop ballads, were issued on tape or record by specialised publishers, thus introducing highly emotional mainstream pop sound to the youth work of (free) churches and Christian associations. Currently, the praise music of the Australian ☉ Hillsong Church, founded in 1983, dominates this field; it operates all over the world and is not only popular but also frequently imitated in the worship songs of mainstream churches and even the WCC.

Praise music marketed in professional quality via YouTube channels and commercial (internet) music distribution (such as that of the ☉ Hillsong Church) corresponds directly to the listening and reception habits of mainstream pop music and thus reduces the shame of being culturally out of touch because of one's religious affiliation. Event-oriented musical religious praise is characterised by easy accessibility, closeness to everyday cultural life and a high degree of participation for large numbers. The fact that this music scene has at the same time become part of the international music business shows its high functionality in the context of a late modern, market oriented form of spirituality tailored to the fulfilment of religious needs, which Hubert Knoblauch, an expert in the sociology of religion, has characterised as "popular religion".

Finally, the "singing priests" in Brazil represent a special phenomenon that has contributed decisively to the charismatisation of the Catholic Church in Latin America. The pop star priest Padre Marcelo Rossi is celebrated as the figurehead of the charismatic renewal movement. With this movement of singing priests, the Catholic Church resists the migration to Pentecostal megachurches with their professional and attractive music.

It should be noted that in addition to this trend towards the globalisation and standardisation of praise music in many countries, there are also developments towards new creative musical experiments, mixing local musical traditions, traditional gospel music or hip-hop with international influences. In many African countries, for example, this "blending" of styles of music and performance is a highly creative contribution to cultural developments that are relevant to society as a whole (Chitando 2002).

The traditional denominational churches have been massively challenged by the praise music scene of the charismatic or Pentecostal → megachurches. In analogy to the discussion about religious hit songs in the 1960s, they have to make it clear which musical forms and traditions – and thus which currents of spirituality – they consciously want to promote and integrate, and which ones they do not approve of, without overestimating their possible influence on the free religious market.

⊙ **Case study: Hillsong**

The name Hillsong stands both for a Pentecostal movement and also for numerous Hillsong congregations worldwide. Since the turn of the century, the Pentecostal Hillsong mega church from Australia has developed into a global network of churches all over the world. They exist in many major European cities – in Germany, for example, they are to be found in 2022 in Constance, Düsseldorf, Munich and Cologne. In Berlin, the "Berlin Connect" church, founded in 2008, has been part of the global Hillsong Church for several years.

The emergence of this successful global network of churches, with its headquarters in Sydney, signalises a new trend: big cities are hotbeds for new forms of global Pentecostal Christianity. What is characteristic of the Hillsong church is that it starts from a common global context rather than from different types of urban context. Hillsong sees itself as a global church. This is reflected, for example, in the fact that church services and other events are predominantly held in English, with simultaneous translations into different languages. In addition, Hillsong churches are multi-ethnic, unlike most other new churches.

Hillsong Church became known in the 1990s, even before it became a church planting movement, through contemporary Christian worship songs. Since then, Hillsong has developed a church concept that includes obligatory formats for praise, for worship services and leadership structures. These are adopted and passed on through the network of churches associated with Hillsong.

Accordingly, all Hillsong services have the same structure. With its combination of excellent bands and the use of media technology, Hillsong offers the experience of an event which is comparable to a pop concert. Theatres and clubs as event venues demonstrate that church can be fun and entertaining. Pastors who are "hip" and "cool" preach in a style reminiscent of motivational speakers, so that the church succeeds in appealing to a young urban audience. Its roots in the revival movement and its conversion-oriented piety are evident in the ritual of the altar call. In every service or meeting, the sermon or catechesis is followed by the call to conversion. The Hillsong Church teaches that personal conversion and subsequent baptism by immersion are indispensable to becoming a Christian.

In addition to the Sunday service "events", the followers are encouraged to attend one or two weekly meetings in small groups. The focus on shared activities, friendship and fun is an important factor in the church's success. People who come for the first time, or are even new to a city, are especially welcomed at Hillsong Church and find it easy to connect with a large network of young people. It is remarkable how Hillsong churches manage to mobilise volunteers to lead church worship or small groups and take on other activities such as music and social media. Getting involved gives volunteers a sense of purpose and of being part of a "bigger picture".

As in many other megachurches, the founders, Brian and Bobby Houston, keep a tight hold on the reins. As global leaders, they preside in Sydney over the church with a board of elders they have appointed themselves. The fact that in Hillsong churches it is not possible to become a formal member reinforces the concept of leadership by recognised spiritual authority, which is typical of charismatic leadership structures. Instead, affiliation to the church is expressed in voluntary work and in the financial contribution requested from those "who consider Hillsong their spiritual home." Despite its Pentecostal roots, Hillsong Church plays down its Pentecostal identity and presents itself as a contemporary church for the 21st century.

Typical Pentecostal practices such as speaking in tongues or laying on of hands are not part of Sunday services, but may occasionally occur in special prayer meetings or seminars.

However, the Pentecostal heritage of the Hillsong Church becomes visible as soon as "family values", sexuality and homosexuality are discussed.

In its mission statement, the Hillsong Church places mission and evangelism at the centre. With its successful founding of churches that particularly attract young people, Hillsong also wants to inspire other churches and invites their pastors to join the Hillsong network. Christians of all denominations are invited via social media to large gatherings such as the annual Hillsong Conferences. The Hillsong churches cooperate with other organisations on a local level, for example with food banks or the Salvation Army, in order to collect and distribute food and gifts at festive seasons.

An important question regarding mission is whether Hillsong Church actually succeeds in reaching non-believers with the gospel. Research shows that most Hillsong visitors were raised as Christians and used to go to church. Hillsong provides an attractive environment for young people to live out their Christianity with modern-style worship services and to make friends easily. One interviewee said: "Hillsong is the reason why I have kept my faith".

3.10 How we lead: Charisms, authority and leadership

Pentecostal-charismatic movements also present themselves in the German-speaking context as international and transconfessional movements for renewal and mission with a complex and diverse appearance. The case is similar with respect to the understanding and practice of leadership. Different forms of leadership are practised in the various forms of Pentecostal-charismatic movements. The ⊙ Association of Pentecostal Churches (BFP), for example, has a synodal and congregational structure. The highest decision-making body is the "Federal Conference", which elects the board members. The accentuation of the autonomy of the local congregation naturally stands in contrast to the search for a common profile. The consequence of the former is that individual congregations only have a limited commitment within the context of the larger church community. The more definitely the varying congregational identities are supposed to be integrated into binding forms of communication, the more reason there is to break out of such structures, for example if a rapidly growing congregation feels that they limit the dynamics of the Pentecostal experience too strongly. There are completely different leadership structures in other cases, for example in the ⊙ Church of God (Cleveland), whose highest legal authority is the "International General Assembly", or in independent Pentecostal-charismatic congregations, which are directed by the vision and work of their founding pastor, assisted by a group of elders.

Characteristic for all expressions of Pentecostal-charismatic movements is the concept of "return to early Christianity" or a "theology of restoration", which is also valid with regard to the understanding and practice of charisms, authority and leadership.

In their various concretions, Pentecostal-charismatic movements refer to the following biblical contexts:
- the preaching of Jesus and the apostles, accompanied by signs, miracles and the casting out of demons (cf. Mt 10:7 ff.; Mk 16:15 ff. a. o.),

- the Pentecost experience reported in Acts and the loving harmony practised within the Early Church (cf. Acts 1 and 2),
- the emergence of certainty of the Spirit through charisms, especially → glossolalia, prophecy and healing (baptism in the Spirit) as well as the pneumatic form of worship in Corinth with its dynamics of hymn and prayer, teaching and revelation, prophecy and speaking in tongues (cf. 1 Cor 12–14 and 1 Cor 14:26 respectively),
- the promise of the Kyrios Jesus in the Johannine farewell discourses that the Spirit sent by the Father will guide his own into all truth (cf. Jn 14–17),
- trust in the leadership of the church through Jesus Christ and his Spirit, who has given it the fivefold ministry: apostles, prophets, evangelists, pastors and teachers (cf. Eph 4:11).

They have distinct reservations towards ritualised forms of worship and juridical fixations of congregational membership. They insist on the immediacy of the Spirit in every believer and accentuate the autonomy of the individual congregation. They are threatened, among other things, by the enthusiastic overestimation of the possession of the Spirit (cf. the controversies with Paul), by a pseudo-prophetic awareness of power, by a piety that is oriented towards the visible and underestimates the challenge and brokenness of Christian life.

Discourses on leadership issues

Discourses on leadership issues play a central role in Pentecostal-charismatic fellowships and contribute to the development and resonance of the movement. Differences and disputes in the understanding and practice of leadership lead to splits. Charismatic authority in Pentecostal-charismatic movements is achieved by the manifestation of spiritual certainty in the charisms, where unusual and extraordinary experiences play an important role. Religious experiences such as visions, → glossolalia, healings, sudden inspirations and miracles lead to initiation into charismatic spirituality. By "removing the taboo on emotional faith" (Heribert Mühlen), strong feelings are evoked, at the same time justifying and demonstrating charismatic authority. In Pentecostal-charismatic groups, Christian religiosity is a fellowship experience with intensive forms of expression that can almost be described as communitarian. It evokes admiration and approval, but also detachment and rejection. Where Christian faith takes on a clear form combined with great personal commitment, there is also the danger of negative effects. Religious devotion can be exploited. Orientation towards charismatic leadership personalities can prevent maturity and growth in the faith. The appeal to the Spirit can be functionalised in favour of a questionable striving for power and dominance. If a group has a strong sense of mission, the result can be an elitist self-centredness that sees the Spirit of God working only within its own ranks. There have recently been controversies about spiritual abuse within the Pentecostal movement, followed by a critical discussion of Pentecostal-charismatic movements both outside and inside the movements themselves, as is evident from recent discussions.

In this situation, a helpful offer for a critical ecumenical dialogue within the Charismatic-Pentecostal scene as well as with it and with other churches was set up by the Evangelical Alliance in Germany (EAD) in 2015 with a contact centre for issues concerning spiritual abuse of power. In the "*Clearingstelle EAD Machtmissbrauch*" (Clearing House EAD Power Abuse) experts in the field of spiritual leadership, psychosocial counselling, pastoral care and coaching can be approached about relevant dangers or controversial cases.[24] A broad definition of spiritual or religious abuse of power forms the background: "Religious abuse of power is when people are pressurised to do something that they would not do of their own accord, and the person exercising pressure has an advantage. In the process, the personal boundaries of the abused person are invaded and violated. [...] In the Christian environment, it often comes additionally to abuse of spiritual themes. People are pressured with spiritual/religious content to do or not to do something, because it benefits the person doing the pressurising. Religious abuse of power takes place in different interpersonal contexts and to various extents. It can be exercised by leaders, colleagues or other members of a group or congregation, whether occasionally or continuously. Of course, the same mechanisms can operate between volunteers and full-time staff."[25] There is a controversial debate about the extent to which the aforementioned Clearing House can effectively fulfil its cause and also de facto successfully settle matters of responsibility for supervision and ecclesiastical discipline. Nonetheless, it is encouraging that in the meantime, both in the area of the Roman Catholic dioceses – partly overlapping with the issue of preventing sexual abuse by church officials – and also in the Protestant free churches, there is a great deal of good material and helpful papers as well as other publications which could further promote the objective discussion on the claims to power and the defence against forms of spiritual abuse of power in churches of different denominational origins.[26]

---

24 https://www.ead.de/kontakt/plattform-religioeser-machtmissbrauch/

25 Cf. ibid. with reference to *Kessler* 2020, 14–15.

26 Cf. on the Catholic side e.g. https://bistum-osnabrueck.de/was-ist-geistlicher-missbrauch; for the debate within the VEF: https://www.baptisten.de/fileadmin/bgs/media/dokumente/Edition-BEFG-Band-4-Verantwortlich-Gemeinde-leiten.pdf. See also *Tempelmann* 2018 and *Johnson/Van Vonderen* 1996.

The understanding of local congregation and church in Pentecostal-charismatic movements starts out from the charismatic experience of individuals and fellowships and can be linked to various organisational structures. Following Walter J. Hollenweger, it can be said that over time the Pentecostal-charismatic movements come to resemble other churches more and more, getting increasingly involved with the institutional dimension which was initially only weakly developed. In recent decades, the Pentecostal movement in Germany has not only been genuinely surprised by the charismatic renewal in the churches. It has also had to accept being overtaken by the independent charismatics, although the latter could have profited from the experience and wisdom of the older Pentecostal movement and thus avoided going down some blind alleys of questionable power-charismatics. Segregation, however, is possibly a principle of propagation in Pentecostal-charismatic movements, which thus contributes to the fragmentation of Protestant Christianity. That is due, among other things, to their strong emphasis on orientation through experience, but also to their church-planting programme. Such structures do not make it easy for other Christian churches to enter into an appropriate relationship with Pentecostal-charismatic movements.

Women's representation in leadership positions is limited, although they have played a significant role in the history of Pentecostalism. Married couples are more likely to take on leadership responsibilities. In tension with the Pauline perspectives on the charismatic church, which is marked by a participatory structure, many churches emphasise the prominent position of the leadership, the pastor and the elders – especially in the growing independent spectrum of Pentecostal-charismatic movements. Accordingly, relationships of authority and authoritative super- and subordinations are emphasised and practised. In some congregations, an official hierarchy is rejected and replaced by a hierarchy of anointing or the nomination of a Senior Pastor, who has the highest authority. The term and attribution "apostolic ministry" is also used for the highest office of leadership, aiming at the restoration of early Christian authority and power that transcends congregations and is oriented towards the foundation of new churches. Leading pastors in → megachurches, whose influence is also growing in the European context, must be competent in rhetoric, suited to the media, qualified for management and skilled in writing – at one and the same time.

Religious and social backgrounds

In pluralistic social cultures, the search for religious identity follows contradictory patterns: on the one hand as an adaptation to processes of individualisation in forms of spiritual self-enhancement, on the other as a protest against modern individualisation by abandoning and renouncing the ego, in some cases in religious groups that expect standardised behaviour from their members. Modern culture is not only determined by individualisation processes. New religious movements pursue counter-cultural accents. Individuals, especially young people, have become decidedly weary of individuality and long for a decrease in decision-making and responsibility. Pentecostal-charismatic movements derive their attractiveness not only from the intensity of their religious experience and their sense of mission, but also from the ambivalences of social modernisation processes and the failing ability of institutionalised Christianity to renew itself. While the systems which protect the institutions of the Christian faith are increasingly called into question nowadays, the significance of "emotionally supported community" (Danièle Hervieu-Léger) for the life of churches and Christians is increasing. Progressive individualisation processes in modern societies lead to paradoxical effects. The need for leadership and guidance becomes stronger, as does the search for confirmation of one's own faith by others. This happens in communities of a manageable size, in which the sharing of Christian faith and life is closely related to one's life story and everyday occurrences. The commitment to a fellowship of one's own choice for a limited period of time creates room for the exchange of experiences, enabling new forms of religious reassurance. Criticism of modernity is also a characteristic of Pentecostal-charismatic forms of fellowship, as is the striving to create a new inculturation of Christianity in the context of modernity and late modernity; here the function of religion as a processing of contingency is just as apparent as the longing for emotionality and experiences of community with a richness of relationships. However, there is also the danger that the "we" of faith is understood in a way that is too narrow and limited, that one is fixated on one particular theme, setting oneself apart from other groups in an elitist fashion, withdrawing into one's own milieu and becoming homogeneous. Homogeneity, however, is not to be recommended as the characteristic of a Christian congregation. Leadership structures that encourage it misjudge the diversity of spiritual activity.

In the present situation, it is important to win back both the spirit and the institution, for it is the combination of both which is indispensable for the Christian faith. The conflict between institution and charisma requires a twofold learning pro-

129

cess: in new situations and challenges, the development of an institution will have to emerge more clearly. At the same time, God's Spirit is not a principle of renewal without a tradition, and newly emerging experiences of the Spirit must be verified by historical continuity.

3.11 Where we are sent: Mission and witness

"Showing what I love – speaking to Muslims about the Christian faith": this is the motto chosen by the EKD Centre for Mission in the Region, the Association of Missionary Services (AMD) and the United Evangelical Mission (VEM) in order to encourage Christians to meet up with Muslims "with respect and on an equal footing"[27]. When asked whether it is in order for Christians to talk about their faith, Sven Lager, the Christian director of the Refugio refugee facility of the Berlin City Mission, says something which is typical for the spirit of Scripture: "To testify to my Christian faith is only possible with love – and if I am willing to see how God works in others. I say: 'In you I meet God'. That's when the ice breaks" (op. cit., 6).

There is now open reflection on the topic of mission in the traditional denominational churches, whether Protestant or Catholic. This was not always the case. For a long time after 1945, it was this topic which distinguished the free churches from the historical churches. The latter were firmly founded on infant baptism and their established church structures, passing

---

27 See the handout with the original title: https://www.a-md.de/fileadmin/user_upload/Kommunikation/Allgemein/Handreichung_Zeigen_was_ich_liebe_final_screen.pdf.

on religious tradition in families, schools and society at large; they had little reason to go in search of new church members through active missionary efforts outside their traditional territories. The free churches were quite different: they only baptised those who were able to confess their personal faith, and this was organically linked to the propagation of faith, meaning mission. The background to these different attitudes towards mission is not only connected with the theology of baptism, but is also historically based.

From the middle of the 19th century onwards, "foreign mission" was distinct from the "home mission" of J.H. Wichern and others, which deepened popular faith through social work. In the colonial era before 1914, mission abroad was even one of the most important topics for the historical denominational churches. Missionary societies were founded, which led to the expansion of the European denominations all across the globe, but this often led to the export of specific cultural characteristics and problems of the mother churches and their countries to other parts of the world. In many parts of the world, Christianity with its own roots was only able to flourish after it had broken away from the influences of the European mission. Even where Christianity had already existed as an indigenous entity outside Europe before the age of mission, the confrontation with the colonial heritage of the mission churches played no small role. In the second half of the 20th century, firstly as a result of saturation of the established churches and later thanks to a gradually growing attitude of post-colonial self-criticism, the topic of mission was considered to be a speciality of the free churches or else it was limited to revival groups in the mainstream German churches. Yet this distinction only represents one side of the issue.

On the other hand, the historical background described above has to be kept in mind in order to understand the considerable development in missiology that took place in the same period of the 20th century, when there was a strong emphasis on the *Missio Dei*, i.e. God's own mission, which God himself – not the church – fulfils in the world. It is precisely the divine preponderance in all mission that allows the Church to be missionary, at the same time planting the seed of the gospel in soil that has already been prepared by other convictions and cultures and which must not be trampled underfoot if the seed is to grow. Missiology used to speak in terms of the "inculturation" of the gospel in new contexts or its "convivence" (meaning "living together") with other religions, but nowadays such expressions have been largely replaced by the term "intercultural theology" in the relevant faculties and specialist publications. Thus the concept of mission has receded into the background, but the factual issue has come (back) into the centre of the established churches. This should characterise the situation today.

In the broader reality of the German Protestant church, the Synod of the EKD in Leipzig in 1999 formed a turning point, putting the mission issue back on the agenda. At this synod, the theologian Eberhard Jüngel held a lecture in which he described mission as the "heartbeat" of the church. He used the analogy of systole and diastole to emphasise that the church must first open up to receive the gospel, in order to pass it on in a second step as mission. For Jüngel, this went hand in hand with the fact that the church does not first have to declare that the world, as addressee of its mission, is a "stronghold of darkness", in order then to present the gospel as the saving "light of the world".

It is perhaps a coincidence that this defining lecture was held in 1999, shortly before the turn of the millennium, but the apocalyptic echoes in the contrast between the "light of the world" and the "stronghold of darkness" are no coincidence, but highly significant for an appreciation of the mission theme, especially with regard to the Pentecostal churches. The experiences with the workings of the Holy Spirit, which form an essential starting point for Pentecostalism, have repeatedly strengthened the consciousness in Pentecostal congregations that they are living at the end of the age, when all things will come to an end. This idea derives from the biblical prophecy in Joel 2, which foresees the outpouring of the Spirit upon people of all ages as an eschatological sign. Mass revivals following on the Pentecostal missionary movement, which spread throughout established networks of Protestant missionary organisations in the early 20th century, were seen as evidence of the imminent return of Christ and increased the sense of urgency for mission. This Pentecostal conviction has no real counterpart in the mainstream churches, but the fact that the imminent end of the world intensifies the urgency of mission is also felt by many traditional denominational churches, following biblical texts such as 2 Peter 3. The biblical argumentation in this chapter, which is characterised by apocalyptic imagery, concentrates on God's long-suffering in delaying the end of the world, allowing time for all people to hear of the gospel, which is then seen as a safe refuge at the Last Judgement.

It is probably this very pointed (exactly: apocalyptic) pragmatism, demanding a "take it or leave it" decision, that has given mission a bad press in some church circles to this day and has repeatedly led to the suggestion of fairly implausible alternatives like "mission or dialogue". But as already mentioned at other places in this document, an apocalyptic way of thinking does not necessarily determine what is to be thought with its help. Leaving aside dualistic models and highly exaggerated expectations of the end of the world, the insight still remains, and is probably both acceptable and important to all Christians, that the gospel prevails against the horrors of the end of the world, since its propagation helps to prevent fear and terror from spreading in the world. The gospel radiates like light in the world, effortlessly bringing clarity, because in its light everything *becomes* clear. In this sense, mission is a driving force of various Christian congregations, both in the historical denominations and in the Pentecostal environment.

After the Pentecostal movement, like many other movements before it, has had to adjust to the absence of the parousia (return of the Risen Christ), the mission discussion – as in many evangelical churches – concentrated primarily on effective methods and strategies of mission and community development, but mission still remained a central aspect. For example, in the Pentecostal church federation founded by Karl Fix in Berlin in 1934, which is now mainly represented in Württemberg, the mission priority is already expressed in the title: "Volksmission entschiedener Christen". The purpose of a missionary congregation was "to pray for people who live in sin and bondage and also in sickness, and thus to save their lives in body, soul and spirit". To this day, many Pentecostal ministries and charismatic congregations have the term "mission" in their names. At the same time, the term "evangelisation" is taking the place of the word "mission". Some Pentecostal networks also consciously dispense with the controversial term "mission".

The presence of the kingdom of God on the one hand, its proclamation here and now and the diaconal action of the church working towards its fulfilment, forms a contrast on the other hand to its perfect realisation, awaited but unattainable, at a time when crying and tears will be no more. This is a basic theme of mission, both in Pentecostal mission theology and that of other denominations. In continuity with the beginnings of the Pentecostal movement, Pentecostal theologians today also emphasise that the Pentecostal gifts of the outpouring of the Holy Spirit – such as speaking in tongues, but also healing and justice – are a clear expression of the fact that the kingdom of God has already dawned. Here we find a fundamental agreement with the view that guides many churches of the historical confessions, for example, that the church is the eschatological foretaste of the kingdom of God in the world (Oscar Cullmann) and that the mission of the church conveys this foretaste. In the words of Jürgen Moltmann: "The creative and life-giving Spirit of God brings eternal life here, now, before death – not just after death [...]. Understood in this divine sense, mission is nothing other than a movement of life and healing."[28]

One question that results from this and that contains various possible answers is: how does the Holy Spirit signalise the kingdom of God in the here and now – by growth, by sudden outbreaks, or both? While Jürgen Moltmann, for example, emphasises growth more strongly, taking the immanent presence of the Spirit in life for granted, Frank Macchia assumes that the

28 *Jürgen Moltmann*, Pentecostal Theology of Life, in: Journal of Pentecostal Theology 9 (1996), 3–15, cited in *Haustein/Maltese* 2014, 452 f.

Spirit intervenes "as an omnipotent and alien mystery that miraculously breaks in, roaring like a mighty wind".[29]

The notion of "breaking in" describes the power of the Spirit to act, which under certain circumstances can also change the direction of the mission. At the same time, the attribution of power to act can be understood as an interpretation of the *Missio Dei* that responds to the human idea of feasibility with a certain humility.

The acceptance of the work of the Holy Spirit – whether as growth, as breaking-in or both – leads to further questions which need to be addressed in ecumenical dialogue with Pentecostal churches and Pentecostal theologians, but not with them alone. These include, for example, the question of the understanding of the world: is it seen, in a dualistic view, as the scene of a battle between the worldly powers of darkness and the shining power of the Holy Spirit? Concepts of a"spiritual warfare", that are as common in some Pentecostal churches as the Calvinist-influenced view that the world is a testing ground for faith, reflect the basic sense of threat mentioned above. A similar dualistic worldview can also be seen in the WCC mission statement "Together for Life" (2012), which contrasts the global economy and its devastating effects with the Spirit of God and the commitment to justice and solidarity.[30] How can this dualistic notion and basic sense of threat be reconciled with the doctrine of the good creation upon which God has poured out his Spirit?

---

29 *Frank Macchia*, The Spirit and the Life: A Further Response for Jürgen Moltmann, in: Journal of Pentecostal Theology 5 (1994), 121–127, 122, cited in Haustein/Maltese 2014, 455.

30 https://www.oikoumene.org/de/resources/documents/together-towards-life-mission-and-evangelism-in-changing-landscapes.

⊙ Case study: Pentecostal Korean congregations in Germany

The Pentecostal movement in South Korea can be mainly traced back to the founding of the ⊙ Yoido Full Gospel Church (*Sunbogeum*), which began under the leadership of Pastor David Yonggi Cho and Pastor Ja Shil Choe in the late 1950s. What started with open-air services for children and tent crusades with a small number of visitors from poor backgrounds developed over the decades into a Pentecostal movement – the Full Gospel Church Pentecostalism – which has had a profound impact on Christian self-understanding and also on society in Korea. Today, the Yoido Full Gospel Church, with its headquarters in Seoul and its 800,000 members, is the largest single church in the world.

According to statistics from 2019, 680 missionaries are working for the Yoido Full Gospel Church in 64 countries, and 1,171 congregations with a total of over 100,000 members have been planted. As early as 1975, the Full Gospel Church World Mission Center was founded in accordance with the motto "We spread out the Pentecostal Holy Spirit movement to all nations". In Europe, the missionary activity of the Yoido Full Gospel Church began in 1976 on the initiative of Korean nurses in Germany who had already come into contact with the Yoido Full Gospel Church. They gathered in their hostels to listen to tapes of Pastor Yonggi Cho's sermons. More and more Koreans joined these self-organised communities. In 1974, the first Korean Full Gospel Church was founded in Berlin. Further congregations followed in Cologne, Dinslaken, Bonn and Düsseldorf, all of which still exist today. There are now eleven Full Gospel Church congregations in Germany, organised under the umbrella of the Full Gospel Church Europe Mission Society.

We can illustrate the history of Yoido Full Gospel Church congregations in Germany by taking the Yoido Full Gospel Church Düsseldorf as an example. In 1974, seven believers under the leadership of a Korean pastor held the first worship service in the chapel of the Düsseldorf University Hospital. Since then, the congregation has moved several times and grown considerably. After a short period as subtenants in a German Pentecostal church, they acquired their own premises in an apartment block in 1981. Since 2003, the congregation has its own church building that previously belonged to a Protestant congregation. Today, the Full Gospel Church Düsseldorf has around 400 members and is one of the largest free churches in Düsseldorf. It was one of the first Korean congregations to organise German-language Christian events for the second generation of Korean Christians. A significant initiative in 2007 was the introduction of a German-language service led by a German-speaking Korean pastor. This service was later called *Church Plus,* focusing on mission to German-speaking visitors and later developing into an international community within the Korean congregation. Basically, the congregation is similar to the mother church Yoido in that it wants to win people for the faith and the church. There are simultaneous translations of the Korean main service for non-Korean visitors, children are encouraged to bring their friends (also non-Korean ones) to the service, there are mission-oriented concerts, lectures or events in old people's homes and hospitals, and *Church Plus* appeals to an international audience. The Düsseldorf congregation is also involved in mission projects in various countries such as India, Romania, Hungary and the Central African Republic.

Trust in the work of God's Spirit in the world has received more and more attention in the World Council of Churches in the last two decades, thanks to the growing influence of Pentecostal and Orthodox Christians. For example, at the World Mission Conference in Athens in 2005 the distinct inclusion of the Holy Spirit in the understanding of mission contributed to a change of attitude, leading away from a "messianic" mission, which places a high value on the contribution of human beings to the realisation of God's kingdom, towards a more humble and "pastoral" mission.[31] The plea for the work of the Holy Spirit in the title of the Athens Conference – "Come, Holy Spirit, heal and reconcile" – challenges human notions of feasibility and places its trust in the transforming power of the Holy Spirit.

There is no doubt that in connection with mission some topics, and above all practices, cause irritation and make it difficult to hold an unprejudiced ecumenical conversation about mission with representatives of Pentecostal churches, but also with free churches and sometimes even the established denominations. In the course of the influx of refugees from Syria, Afghanistan and Iran since 2014, the topic of baptism and mission has also led to controversies within the historical-confessional churches. Other sensitive issues are proselytism and any form of mission that puts pressure on the other. Here too, however, it is not enough to draw the lines of conflict one-dimensionally between historical-confessional churches on the one hand and free churches, Pentecostal churches and charismatic movements on the other. Regional differences often play a central role in the understanding of mission. Many historical-confes-

---

31 *Jacques Matthey*, Some Reflections on the Significance of Athens 2005, in: EMS (ed.), Vom Geist bewegt – zu verwandelnder Nachfolge berufen. Zur Weltmissionskonferenz in Tansania, Hamburg 2018, 11–29, 13.

sional churches in the Global South, for example, have a more active understanding of mission than was the case in the established church situation in Germany for a long time. In addition, contextual religious factors such as the numerical ratio of Christians to members of other religions or questions of local religious dominance influence the understanding of mission.

In many areas, ecumenical dialogue has already achieved progress and clarification. With regard to the proselytising of Christians from other denominations, the World Missionary Conference in Edinburgh in 1910 brought about an initial agreement in the end. Since the multitude of partly competing missionary societies was threatening the credibility of the Christian witness at the beginning of the 20th century, there was already a striving for unity at that time, also and especially in mission. To this day, the struggle for unity in mission is the central topic at world mission conferences, in which representatives of Pentecostal churches are now actively involved. This was also emphasised at the last world mission conference in Arusha/Tanzania in 2018 by the general secretary of the World Council of Churches (WCC), Olav Fykse Tveit, in his opening address: "Care for the mission of the church has always been driving force behind the ecumenical movement, toward our common witness and service, and therefore also toward new insights and new commitments. In the WCC, which also included the International Missionary Council since the 3rd Assembly in New Delhi in 1961, the call to be one has always been inspired by the call to mission."[32]

---

32 https://www.oikoumene.org/resources/documents/opening-address-of-wcc-general-secretary-rev-dr-olav-fykse-tveit.

With regard to the issue of missionary practices and strategies, an ecumenical milestone was reached in 2011 with the document "Christian Witness in a Multi-Religious World". Here the Pontifical Council for Interreligious Dialogue, the World Evangelical Alliance and the WCC agreed on a "code of conduct" which considers any psychological pressure or even physical manipulation and violence to be incompatible with the spirit of the gospel and which sees respect for the freedom and dignity of others as the basic prerequisite for dialogue and missionary witness[33]. Numerous representatives of Pentecostal churches and charismatic movements were involved in this process, as well as in the reception process carried out in Germany under the title "Mission Respect"

Ecumenical rapprochements were also achieved with regard to the provocative issue of witness and service, which led to the break within the WCC and the founding of the Lausanne Movement in 1974. The Cape Town Commitment adopted by the Lausanne Congress for World Evangelisation in 2010, which emphasises, alongside witness, the pointedly active and ethical character of true Christian life, is an expression of ecumenical rapprochement[34].

There is one topic that repeatedly leads to controversy at Protestant church synods, in official statements on interreligious dialogue by churches or the WCC, and in many other formal or informal places: what is the relationship between mission and interreligious dialogue? One particularly controversial issue in this context is the mission to the Jews. On the one hand, critics of colonialism fear a repetition of colonial strategies of oppres-

---

33 https://www.oikoumene.org/de/resources/documents/christian-witness-in-a-multi-religious-world.
34 https://lausanne.org/content/ctc/ctcommitment#capetown.

sion of "the others" and a revival of Christianity's claim to absoluteness; their opponents on the other side see the abstention
from mission as a betrayal of the gospel commission, or simply
as a neglect of the necessity to speak of one's heartfelt persua-
sion. In addition, there are people who fear the collapse of the
Western world if mission is abandoned in favour of dialogue. "By
their fruits you shall know them" is the concise form of the response by one of the best-known Pentecostal theologians, Amos
Yong, to the question of whether the Spirit of God also blows in
other religions. The criteria for the working of this blowing of
the Spirit of God are evident, even if in individual cases it has to
be disputed over and over again, leading to discussion and argu-
ment. But it is nevertheless the kingdom of justice, peace, hope
and love that is proclaimed by the Spirit of God.

3.12 What unites us: Pentecostal churches and ecumenism

Unity in meeting face to face, listening and sharing "stories" –
personal experiences as a Christian in different contexts – is
one of the basic elements of the ecumenical movement. Personal encounter is formative and reduces distance without removing differences. Ecumenical encounter includes celebration
in prayer, song, dance or on a pilgrimage: unity is experienced
here on a comprehensive level – both sensory and rationally.

"Everyone should pray in his or her own language of the heart!"
Everyone who has participated in a service in the context of
worldwide ecumenism will recognise this summons to pray – for
example the Lord's Prayer – in one's native tongue. Hearing the
language medley that follows, it is not only noticeable that the

Spanish speakers are among the fastest, while the German ones tend to bring up the rear. Praying together also creates communion: the joint practice unites, despite the diversity of languages.

The search for a communion that embraces diversity is a special characteristic of the Pentecostal movement. From the very beginning, Pentecostal churches have faced the challenge of finding unity between different groupings from Methodist and Wesleyan churches, the Holiness Movement, Reformed churches, the Anglican Communion, Baptists, Brethren and other Christian traditions brought together by a common experience of the Holy Spirit in the early 20th century. Rejection and disaffiliation forced the first Pentecostal churches to establish their own fellowships, often in stark contrast to their original self-understanding as a cross-denominational movement for unity and renewal in all churches. As a result, the ecumenical mindset of Pentecostalism led both to continuity and to discontinuity with different Christian doctrines, practices, rituals, ministries and spiritual disciplines, so that today one cannot speak of a homogeneous communion of churches. The ecumenical history of the Pentecostal churches is of fundamental importance in order to arrive at a theological orientation of the ecumenical potential of the worldwide movement.

What is constitutive for the emergence of the ecumenical movement at the beginning of the twentieth century is that overcoming the divisions between the churches and striving for unity was understood at the same time as a *gift* of God and a *commission* of the churches. It is significant that both movements – Ecumenism and Pentecostalism – emerged parallel to each other in time, and that both are trans-confessional movements for unity and renewal. It was precisely at the transition from the 19th to the 20th century that the idea of a "spiritual church" was born in the historical churches, something separate from the institutionalised church which would transform the denominational differences. The fact that spirit-led and institutional ideas of unity emerged simultaneously in the established churches can probably be explained by the historical circumstances of nationalism and colonialism, which strongly influenced the self-understanding of the historical churches and led to paradoxical concurrent developments. On the one hand, confessionalism gained strength in some places in the 19th century. On the other hand, the mission understanding of the historical churches, which was not infrequently coloured by the imperialistic culture, meant that church unity could only be thought of and practised in the long term on the basis of an open debate with and between the denominations.

The fact that the Pentecostal movement hardly took part in the ecumenical movement at all for a long time has several reasons. On the one hand, it saw itself as interdenominational. On the other hand, its understanding of the church was and is fundamentally different from that of the churches traditionally involved in the ecumenical movement. In addition, the mutual experiences of the churches in the ecumenical movement and the Pentecostal groups led to an estrangement between them, making them suspicious of each other. Members of the Pentecostal movement who were active in ecumenism were viewed with suspicion within their own ranks, and there was little interest in rapprochement on the part of official ecumenical institutions. This changed in the 1990s at the latest, partly through the groundwork of ecumenically committed individuals on both sides.

The trans-confessional understanding of unity in the early Pentecostal movement at the beginning of the 20th century was primarily based on the experience of the outpouring of the Holy Spirit in all kinds of denominations. It was seen as a sign of the imminent unity of all Christians which had already come to fruition through the fellowship in Spirit-baptism and the gifts of the Spirit. The optimism among Pentecostals was underpinned by a firm grasp of the significance of the movement itself. Important for the new movement was the Pentecostal vision of the unity of all churches through the one Spirit of God poured out on the world at Pentecost. This self-understanding, which was ecumenical in principle, interpreted the events of the day of Pentecost in optimistic eschatological expectation of the complete realisation of the Kingdom of God, already manifested in the present spiritual unity of all believers.

This optimism was far removed from a romanticised idea of abstract spiritual unity. Underlying these efforts was the formation of a Pentecostal self-understanding in the sense of a spiritual reality that finds expression in worship, service and fellowship. Pentecostal churches were therefore often reluctant to adopt the title "church" or "denomination" for themselves or the movement as a whole, and criticised the "institutionalism", "formalism", and "denominationalism" among existing churches. The prevailing institutional patterns were criticised because Pentecostals viewed "the Church" fundamentally as an eschatological, not a constituted community. The apparent trend towards denominational separation, inherent in the names of the various churches, contradicted their eschatological and ecumenical expectations. An individual church, denomination or even the Pentecostal movement as a whole were seen as transitory and were to be surpassed by the continuing outpouring of the Holy Spirit and the resulting restoration of Christian unity.

⊙ Case study: Transnational Chinese True Jesus Church

Throughout Germany, there are several dozen Chinese Christian congregations and around a hundred Chinese Bible groups open to the public, mainly in large cities and university towns. In general, these congregations seek contact with the German church even less than other migrant congregations. They also operate in mainland China, where they are also independent of existing church structures. Conversely, they are actively connected with networks of Chinese churches and denominations all over the world. They are often supported financially from Canada or the USA, and there is cooperation in matters of theology and staffing with Hong Kong, Taiwan and Singapore. These transnational networks of Chinese Christians are mostly evangelical or Pentecostal-charismatic.

A clear Pentecostal self-understanding, combined with a global denominational structure, characterises the "True Jesus Church" (*Zhen ye su jiao hui*). In Germany, this church is currently represented by three congregations: in Mannheim, Mönchengladbach and Hamburg. Its name indicates a Christian claim to absoluteness that sounds non-ecumenical, even sectarian, but this can only be understood in the light of history.

Nowhere in the world did the churches and missions of Europe and North America invest so much money and personnel as in China between 1860 and 1950. At the beginning of the 20th century, when anti-colonial uprisings and national movements increasingly set the agenda in China, Protestantism in China seemed to be a foreign body from abroad. Notable hospitals and educational institutions, as well as a dense network of social and charitable institutions, were

Protestant, but foreign-funded and foreign-run, while there was only scant growth in the number of local Christians.

In this complex situation, countless local congregations with no contact to foreign missions suddenly emerged in the first two decades of the 20th century. This is the root cause of what became official government and national church policy after Mao's revolution, namely the prohibition of foreign influence in religious affairs and the propagation of a Chinese Christian identity.

The largest evangelical church to emerge from this indigenisation movement was the *Little Flock*, and the largest Pentecostal church was the True Jesus Church (TJC). Both grew rapidly and by 1950 accounted for more than one-fifth of all evangelical Christians in China, with the True Jesus Church alone accounting for 14 percent. As a church of uneducated peasants, it had to assert itself against the Christian elites in the cities, who profited from foreign education, who could score points with progressive ideas and a modern health system and benefited from political protection. The True Jesus Christians defended their fellowship with the battle cry "But we are the true followers of Jesus!" and developed a correspondingly proud self-confidence.

Apart from its Chinese self-sufficiency, three elements contributed particularly to the profile of the True Jesus Church: the practice of faith healing (for people with completely inadequate health care), praying in tongues in all services (practised by people who were not very eloquent and had little to say in everyday life) and the biblical tradition of the Sabbath. The fact that the True Jesus Church celebrates its services on Saturday has given it a firm and lasting "trade mark" globally over the course of time.

The TJC is globally coordinated by an "International Assembly" with headquarters and office in the USA. Its most important Chinese training centre is in Taiwan, where it is one of the largest churches in the country. Today, there are TJC congregations in 61 countries in Africa and Latin America, and also Russia.

In mainland China, True Jesus churches continue to exist today – partly as independent, unregistered churches, partly in the network of the Chinese Christian Council (the only state-recognised umbrella organisation of Protestant churches). In some places there is a church under the authority of the Christian Council, which holds two services: one on Saturday for Christians of the True Jesus tradition, and one on Sundays for Christians of other traditions, both led by the same pastor. At the Theological Seminary in Nanjing, the national training centre of the Christian Council, there are also Christians from the TJC among the students, and one lecturer in the current teaching staff comes from the TJC in Fujian province.

In 1979, the first TJC Christians from Taiwan came to Germany to study, celebrating their Chinese services on Saturday. That was in Heidelberg. In 1987 the congregation registered as an association, and in 2019 it moved to Mannheim. In addition to the congregations in Mönchengladbach and Hamburg, there are others located in Salzburg and Vienna as well as house groups in Switzerland. They meet on a supra-regional basis for annual Bible seminars, camps, youth camps, etc. In the meantime, members from Germany are increasingly supporting the work of the TJC congregations in Spain, Italy and Greece as well as the house groups which are slowly forming in Eastern Europe.

The congregation in Mannheim holds two one-hour services every Saturday, with a lunch break and meeting time in between. After a song and a time of prayer in tongues or normal language, there is a sermon or a Bible study. To finish the service, another song is sung and there is congregational prayer in tongues. If necessary, the sermon is translated from Chinese into German. Afterwards, there is an extended prayer group, in which everyone can bring in their personal prayer needs and topics. On Saturday evenings, there is a special programme for young people over 18, which they organise themselves. Sometimes the day ends with a fellowship supper.

For TJC Christians, baptisms are only valid if they are administered to adults in "living", i.e. running, water by immersion. The Lord's Supper is celebrated with unleavened bread. TJC members are not allowed to participate in holy communion of other Christian churches. The ritual of foot washing is also practised and is considered a sacrament.

As a transdenominational movement for unity and renewal in all churches, the Pentecostal movement focused on unity in spirit, fellowship and action, but remained oriented towards the autonomy of each individual congregation. The ecumenical movement had a different approach, concentrating on structural processes, bringing representatives of the established church to a binding cooperation and dialogue with each other and attempting to refrain from ecclesial judgements about other denominations and elitist self-descriptions. This concept, which dominated the ecumenical movement, meant that the young and volatile Pentecostal congregations, which had not yet found their feet in the existing church landscape and did not want to form a denomination of their own, were at first not interested in the ecumenical movement as a whole, so that for a long time only individuals were invited to ecumenical meetings. The World Missionary Conference in Edinburgh in 1910 was not aware of the Pentecostal revivals, or regarded them with scepticism rather than giving them space. The optimism that accompanied the birth of the modern Pentecostal movement was thus soon followed by exclusion. This rejection was reinforced by the unprecedented growth and worldwide expansion of the Pentecostal movement, which strengthened feelings of competition rather than interest in cooperation.

Within the Pentecostal movement, growth and differentiation led to the question of permanence, institutional continuity, organisation and structure of the movement. The consequence is a disparate appearance of the Pentecostal churches. On the one hand, the Pentecostal movement – despite the ecumenical vision of a Spirit-led, cross-denominational unity – soon entered the scene of Protestant denominationalism and adapted to the traditional church types, so that today there is a great number of Pentecostal denominations, often differing in doctrine and theological practice. On the other hand, they soon formed into an independent, globally networked church movement that goes far beyond the traditional church boundaries, theological ideals and eschatological expectations of the original renewal movements. What is still missing, however, due to the long exclusion and alienation from the ecumenical movement, is acknowledged by Pentecostal theologians today, namely a Pentecostal ecclesiology that requires dialogue with other churches in order to develop.

The relationship between Pentecostal congregations and churches on the one hand and the ecumenical movement on the other did not change until the second half of the 20th century, when the charismatic movement sparked new experiences of the Holy Spirit in the historical churches. Some representatives of the new generations of classical Pentecostals and the so-called neo-Pentecostals consolidated their efforts to participate in organised ecumenical activities. The development of Pentecostal academic theology and training also helped to equip Pentecostal churches theologically for participation in ecumenical dialogues and to revise the often prevailing opinion that Pentecostals disdained theological, intellectual and ecumenical endeavours. Official and semi-official collaboration of Pentecostal churches in national church councils and ecumenical commissions, as well as the awarding of scholarships worldwide, have helped to establish closer contact with Pentecostal churches and to broaden the basis and support for ecumenical activities. The interest in charismatic spirituality and practice among the established churches, especially in the form of the charismatic renewal movement, has further opened Pentecostal churches for worldwide ecumenical recognition.

An important impulse for ecumenical dialogue with Pentecostal churches is the rediscovery of the spiritual and relational dimension of that which unites Christians. It is therefore no coincidence that spirit-related title themes of WCC assemblies are often formulated as petitions: "Come, Holy Spirit, renew the whole creation" (WCC assembly in Canberra 1991) or "Come, Holy Spirit, heal and reconcile" (World Mission Conference in Athens 2005). Despite all the necessary adherence to the prophetic mission of the churches, the renewal of all creation, healing and reconciliation are not seen as dependent on the actions of churches and Christian communities. The request for the work of the Holy Spirit resists the temptation of a "God-is-with-us" (and not with the others) spirituality and bids a salutary farewell to the idea that human beings can and should bring about the kingdom of God on earth.

This impulse can even be seen as calling Christian universalism into question generally, as has recently been the case in post-colonial critique. Some see this as a fundamental criticism of the ecumenical search for unity, asking whether one may today justifiably speak of unity, common values, a cosmopolitan vision of a united humanity – and if so, under what premises? Does the experience of colonialism not demonstrate that visions of supposedly common humanistic Christian values have failed, because they were in reality tools of imperial cultural adaptation? Can the Christian credo avoid suffering the same fate? One contributing factor is that the tension between unity and diversity is not easy to resolve. Questions arise concerning the controlling power of interpretation and action – who is "the ecumenical subject"? There is potential here for strongly divisive tension. To be sure, unity was never intended to mean denominational or cultural egalitarianism. On the contrary, especially in recent times, difference has been seen as a central and enlivening factor of unity – for example in the model of ecumenism of difference. Nevertheless, one must ask oneself whether a mutual "recognition factor" between Christians is not indispensable and whether their credo is not based on the belief that this is also possible. The traditional Reformation churches see the preaching in accordance with the gospel and the churches' mutual recognition of baptism and holy communion as the foundation and expression of this. The traditional models of unity are particularly criticised in the Global South as being too dogmatic, too far oriented to texts and not far enough to experience, physicality or the Spirit, as too "Eurocentric" and too little open for alternative forms of knowledge. In this situation, Pentecostal churches and charismatic movements form a unique bridge between the Global North and the Global South, where Pentecostal churches have a much stronger presence and also represent the centre of gravity of Christianity today.

⊙ Case study: Church of Pentecost, Ghana

The origins of the *Church of Pentecost* (CoP) in Ghana can be traced to the Apostolic Church of the Gold Coast and Rev. James McKeown (1900–1989), an Apostolic missionary of the Apostolic Church in Bradford, England. At the invitation of Rev. Peter Anim, a prominent local and independent church leader, McKeown came to the Gold Coast (now Ghana) in 1937 to begin his missionary work. After modest beginnings and conflicts that led to separation from both the Apostolic Mission and his home church, McKeown founded the Church of Pentecost in 1962. Its theological principles resembled those of the classical Pentecostal churches. It taught justification by faith in Christ, sanctification as a continuing work of grace by the Holy Spirit, divine healing through the atoning work of Christ, the baptism in the Holy Spirit, initially evidenced by speaking in tongues, and the imminent return of Christ. McKeown founded the church from the outset as an indigenous church whose structures and practices, including funding, corresponded to the indigenous population. His concept followed the idea of the self-supporting, self-propagating and self-governing church.

In 1980, the CoP founded the Pentecostal Social Services (PENSOS) to improve the living conditions of its members and to strengthen the church's contribution to the socio-economic development of the nation. This was to be done primarily in the areas of education and health. Today, the CoP runs 84 primary schools, three vocational schools and two secondary schools. The Pentecost University was founded in 2003. In the health sector, the church established two hospitals and seven health centres. In the wake of the Covid-19 pandemic in 2020, the CoP made its multi-purpose Pentecost Convention Centre on the outskirts of Accra available free of charge to the Ghanaian government for the accommodation and treatment of infected persons. The CoP is also involved in the areas of community development and microfinance. Since 2012, it has played an important role in the National Peace Council (NPC), which was founded by the Ghanaian parliament in 2011 to resolve conflicts and secure long-term peace in the country.

The CoP took up its first ecumenical relations outside the Pentecostal churches under the Fourth Chairman, Apostle Michael Ntumy (1998–2008), who worked with the Christian Council of Ghana to coordinate opportunities of national interest. Under the leadership of the Fifth Chairman, Apostle Prof. Opoku Onyinah (2008–2018), ecumenical cooperation was further strengthened. Thus, the church tried to build bridges between the denominations in the country: as chairman of the Ghana Pentecostal and Charismatic Council (GPCC), Apostle Onyinah initiated the signing of a memorandum of understanding with the Christian Council of Ghana to cooperate on issues of church and national interest. At the international level, the CoP participated in the Lausanne Congress in Cape Town in 2010 and became a member of the Pentecostal World Fellowship in 2011.

As for its relations to the WCC, the CoP under the chairmanship of Apostle Ntumy hosted a consultation of the Commission on World Mission and Evangelisation (CWME) on Faith, Healing and Mission in Accra in 2002. From 2002 to 2007, Apostle Onyinah served on this commission as a consultant on Pentecostalism. He has been a member of the Commission from 2007 to the present. Since 2019, Apostle Onyinah has represented the CoP in the ongoing international dialogue between Lutherans and Pentecostal churches. The CoP has been involved in the) Global Christian Forum since the 2nd World Assembly in Manado, Indonesia in 2011. The CoP's ecumenical cooperation was further underscored in June 2017 when it hosted a → Global Christian Forum consultation on "The Church's Call to Mission and Perceptions of Proselytism". Another significant step was the invitation of the Catholic Archbishop of Accra, Charles Palmer-Buckle, to the 13th Extraordinary Council Meeting of the Church held at the Pentecost University College in Accra in 2012. Apostle Onyinah represented the CoP in the sixth phase of the international Catholic-Pentecostal dialogue from 2010 to 2015.

In religious statistics, the CoP stands out because it has spread to all parts of the country and its membership is steadily growing. In 1987 – at the time when McKeown handed over the leadership of the church to a Ghanaian in the person of Apostle S.F. Safo – the CoP was registered for the first time as the fastest growing church in the country. Four years later, in 1991, an update of the national survey showed that the CoP was already the largest Protestant denomination in Ghana. Currently, the CoP has has about three million members in Ghana, out of a total population of about 30 million. The CoP is now represented in about 100 countries worldwide.

The Pentecostal movement – partly criticising itself for its own transformation as exclusive and confessionalist – calls for reflection on how to formulate an ecumenical self-understanding as a movement among the churches of today. The ecumenical dialogue on unity must start with the question of the respective ecclesiology. The heart of Pentecostal ecclesiology is perhaps closest to the idea of koinonia, which has been developed as a common ecumenical horizon in the multilateral dialogue of the WCC Faith and Order Commission since the 1990s.[35] However, just as church as koinonia manifests itself differently among Pentecostals, depending on the negative or positive influences of certain experiences that have shaped the ecclesial self-understanding of the individual or the denomination, one can also speak in the plural of unity conceptions and ecclesiologies for the whole ecumenical landscape. It is important to consider unity at the local and global level as well as in its various dimensions, discussing it on an equal basis, living and experiencing it, and putting it into practice.

---

35 „Die Einheit der Kirche als Koinonia: Gabe und Berufung", in: *Walter Müller-Römheld* (ed.), Im Zeichen des Heiligen Geistes. Bericht aus Canberra 1991, Frankfurt a.M. 1991, 173–176. „Auf dem Weg zu einer umfassenderen Koinonia. Botschaft der Weltkonferenz", in: *Günther Gassmann/Dagmar Heller* (eds.), Santiago de Compostela 1993. Fünfte Weltkonferenz für Glauben und Kirchenverfassung, Frankfurt a.M. 1994, 213–216.

3.13 Concluding remarks

In twelve thematic sections we have dealt with the theological characteristics of the Pentecostal movement. This journey has led from the relevance of the experience of the Holy Spirit to a concrete, contextual understanding of salvation, healing and sanctification, from an understanding of creative emergence to a strong awareness of powers in opposition to God, invoked as spirits and demons. All this is embedded in the comprehensive confidence in the present power of the Spirit, which can be beseeched and praised in prayer and song, which encourages mission work and ultimately holds out hope for ecumenical understanding between Christians and even among religions in the end. None of the twelve themes proved to be unknown in the reflection on faith practised in the traditional denominational churches – on the contrary: not infrequently, the Pentecostal "ceterum censeo" that God is present poses a challenge for a clearer formulation of faith in the context of the mainstream churches. Above all, however, the twelve thematic approaches can act as an encouragement to embark on a common journey of discovery of the common Christian faith – whilst enduring questioning, criticism, doubts and new discoveries. In its turn, such insights encourage us to gain and appreciate the Pentecostal movement as a strategic partner for overcoming the global crisis, so that our common journey of faith can also become a common search for a planetary ethic of sustainability.

4. Religion – Politics – World Responsibility

4.1 Approaches

The relationship between religion, politics and world responsibility is complex and controversial when applied to the spectrum of Pentecostal and charismatic churches. In ecumenical dialogue, whether on a national or an international level, a thorough scrutiny and a critical discernment of spirits is therefore always necessary. This applies equally to the relationship with churches of other confessional and contextual origins as well as to the dialogue with Pentecostal/Charismatic churches. Sweeping judgments are to be avoided, as well as generalising patterns of recognition, especially when carried over from the German context to others.

This is all the more important as the participants in the dialogue often have deterring examples in their minds: Pentecostal churches that allow themselves to be instrumentalised by autocratic political leaders to justify certain conservative fundamentalist and anti-human rights positions with religious arguments, or even directly support repressive and right-wing populist regimes (South Africa, Brazil, USA under Trump). There is indeed concern in both politics and ecumenical churches that parts of the charismatic-Pentecostal scene are actively contributing to a massive and often anti-ecumenical rollback with regard to the prophetic critical witness of the churches. But there is also concern that Protestantism is becoming increasingly fragmented in its political and ethical positions.

This can be observed in Latin America, for example, where the historical Protestant churches are collapsing more and more, their educational institutions are being weakened and parts of their membership even openly support repressive regimes. Also and especially among historical Protestant Christians, one encounters a high number of so-called "Bolsonaro Christians" (see ⊙ Evangelical Lutheran Church in Brazil).

However, the situation is not uniform in the least; but on the contrary, it is complicated. The trend towards support for repressive regimes can also be observed in a whole range of historically established churches as well as in the evangelical churches. Therefore, the danger of political instrumentalisation should not simply be identified with *one* denominational family. In some African countries, socially committed criticism is now being increasingly voiced by representatives of the more left-wing evangelical spectrum, while some of the historical Protestant churches tend to be closer to the government (and conservative). In addition, there are large Pentecostal/Charismatic churches in Africa that are also critical of the regime, demanding innovations in the area of sustainability and poverty alleviation. Recent research by ethnologists, mission theologians and development scholars has pointed out that some Pentecostal groups are making a relevant contribution to development and that their involvement in issues of social order and stability should not be neglected. In regions where Pentecostal churches predominantly represent small minority groups in an environment dominated by other religions, they need to secure their own existence. In Asia, for example, other religious traditions are more likely to be instrumentalised in the interests of strengthening repressive or autocratic policies (e.g. Hinduism in India, Buddhism in Myanmar or Sri Lanka). In Eastern European and post-Soviet countries the situation is quite heterogeneous. In some countries there are active evangelical or charismatic minority churches whose local congregations do social and charitable work directly with the means at their disposal, while in other churches aggressive Pentecostal missionary activity leads to bitter conflicts.

Thus the picture remains very disparate and inconsistent, for Pentecostal churches are not all alike. A charismatic grassroots church cannot be compared with a globally operating, digitally networked megachurch. A rural Independent Church in the African context (AIC; → African Instituted Churches), which emerged in the context of anti-colonial African self-determination, has little in common with a large, also "independent" but decidedly anti-ecumenical church in the Latin American context, for example the ⊙ Universal Church of the Kingdom of God. The extreme diversity of churches, with their various types and orientations in different continents and contexts, should therefore be taken carefully into account. Even the typology which has often been proposed, which puts the churches into categories – classical Pentecostal, charismatic congregations within denominational churches, neo-Pentecostal and independent – is not adequate to form a manageable framework of criteria and orientation. It is necessary to take a closer, more detailed and context-related look in order to be able to determine which churches are genuinely open to development and ready for dialogue. This is also true with regard to social change. While some churches practise *development from below* and truly contribute to the *empowerment* of the marginalised, others serve to accumulate wealth for a few individual church officials and may indeed be considered a business enterprise disguised as religion.

A more precise perception and analysis of the individual churches within their own context is therefore indispensable. This makes it difficult and demanding to initiate possible dialogue or partnership relationships, but ultimately more promising and ecumenically responsible as long as adequate theologically, ethically and developmentally qualified criteria are applied. One should therefore make use of existing processes and interim results for the assessment of certain Pentecostal/ Charismatic churches, which have often been worked out by regional ecumenical church federations or denominations within their respective areas.

4.2 Paradigm shift: From escaping the world to social ethics

Classically, Pentecostalism was characterised by a type of piety that emphasised the salvation of individual souls from the wicked world (salvation *from* this world), adding them to the chosen "holy remnant".

The eschatological, apocalyptic orientation of classical Pentecostalism to the afterlife corresponded to a basic scepticism of Pentecostal theologians towards critical Western education and science, which tended to be seen as faith-destroying. However, this critical distance to education in some parts of the charismatic-Pentecostal spectrum, for example in the context of the → African Instituted Churches (AIC) with their quite different structures, has to be understood as a consequence of anti-colonial resistance and the rejection of certain colonial influences that were brought in with the Western education system. However, it is noteworthy that changes and shifts of orientation have taken place meanwhile in parts of the charismatic-Pentecostal movement, leading to an openness for a positive view of the world as a place of moral probation as well as to a new interest in questions of social transformation and development (salvation *of* this world). In addition, an academic Pentecostal theology has developed in recent decades in both the Global North and the Global South.

⊙ Case study: Charismatisation in Argentina

Since the 1980s, the non-Catholic religions have expanded strongly in Argentina. In particular, the Protestants, who made up 2.6 percent of the population at the census in 1960, have grown to between 9 and 15 percent of the population today (Pew Research Center 2014). This includes both "mainline" (historical) Protestants and the Pentecostal movement.

Mainline Protestantism (Anglican, Lutheran, Methodist, Presbyterian, Reformed), which came into the country in 1825 with economic migration and rose to the middle class, has been declining since the 1960 s like other mainline churches due to demographic and secular factors. In contrast, charismatic Protestantism has experienced significant growth since the 1980 s (now 75 percent of Protestantism). Promises of salvation in this world and an emotional style of worship appeal especially to members of the lower classes. In poor districts, more than 20 percent of the population are Pentecostal; poverty factors are regularly the reason for converting to Pentecostalism. In the meantime, however, it can be seen that the Pentecostal movement is expanding into the middle class, where it adopts a soft-charismatic and middle-class style.

When combined with charismatic elements, the historical Protestant churches are also an attractive alternative to Pentecostal churches for the middle class. This is evident in various congregations that have adopted a charismatic profile over the course of time. Examples are the Anglican El Buen Pastor Church in an upper middle class neighbourhood of Buenos Aires, and the Scottish Presbyterian Church in Argentina, for example in the Dr Smith Memorial Church in the middle class area Belgrano, which is in the capital. These congregations incorporate Pentecostal elements into their worship, but without the possibly off-putting public speaking in tongues and exorcisms.

In at least some of the Pentecostal churches, a significant movement towards a concretion of the social relevance of the gospel can be discerned, even if it uses to a large extent a different terminology to that of the WCC member churches ("integral mission", "holistic ministries", "social services", "holistic education"). In the meantime, substantial networks for social services, hospitals, rural development programmes and even universities have started and expanded in the Pentecostal spectrum. For this reason, there is a growing need for learning in many Pentecostal churches with regard to professional social and development work, but also on questions of social ethics, and this opens up possible points of contact for dialogue. Some charismatic-Pentecostal churches describe and qualify themselves in part very consciously as factors for sustainable development and the establishment of decent social and living conditions. Many Pentecostal churches show no interest in material support from western development agencies or churches, because they have their own, often quite effective systems of fund-raising and sharing of resources (e.g. through the principle of tithing). Like all churches, however, they probably need expert advice and exchange of expertise in questions of development processes and Christian social ethics.

In South Africa, for example, where the state system is still very weak in the areas of social and health care (80 percent of the population in South Africa have no health insurance) and local economic development (60 percent of the black population is unemployed), Pentecostal churches show initiative with their own culture of enterprise and solidarity and are proving to be important as developers of regional and local prosperity. It could be particularly interesting to enter into a learning partnership with such projects of innovative Christian entrepreneurship, since they do not yet share a common reflection on a Christian corporate or development ethic. Various Pentecostal churches have already created impressive models of an alternative community based on Christian values, which, against the backdrop of increasingly weakening state development programmes, present themselves as flagship projects of an orderly, African modernity or a Christian polity and look to attract further supporters.

In some of the larger Pentecostal churches in South Africa or West Africa the compound usually has a functioning infrastructure. These areas belonging to the church are usually organised as *gated communities*, which means that they have access controls, but guarantee to provide their members with good food, education, health and social security. They are seen even by outsiders as islands of prosperity in an ocean of shortcomings and *bad governance*. Although many churches are accused of financial opacity, they also claim to be more immune to the widespread problem of corruption. In this, at least, they high-light the successes of a Christian Pentecostal social utopia. In the church jargon, these church compounds represent a shining "city on a hill" and are as such part of the mission understanding of such churches. However, the claim to success is still mostly related to the model of an internal group of believers within the denomination and not yet understood in the sense of a community with social, cultural and religious diversity.

⊙ Case study: Pentecostalism in Ethiopia

Protestants of all denominations in Ethiopia are usually referred to as "P'ent'ay", a name derived from the Amharic word for Pentecost. This name, which was originally used derogatorily, is now commonly used by Christians to describe themselves, showing how closely Ethiopian Protestantism is connected with Pentecostal theology and practice. This does not mean, for example, that all Lutherans of the Mekane Yesus Church normally pray in tongues, dance during the church services or abstain from alcohol like Pentecostals. It is rather so, that expressions of Pentecostal piety and theology are found in all Protestant churches, instead of forming barriers between them. In the Ethiopian religious landscape there are only three confessions: Orthodox, Muslim and "P'ent'ay".

This "Pentecostalisation" of Ethiopian Protestantism has developed over the last three decades, accompanied by strong growth of the Protestant churches. While the 1986 census recorded only slightly more than five percent Protestants, their proportion rose to almost 20 percent in the 2007 census and increased to 27 percent in the estimates of the latest Ethiopian Demographic and Health Survey (2019).

Most of this growth has been at the expense of the Ethiopian Orthodox Church, which regards the Pentecostal movement as an "alien" religion to be warded off and suppresses charismatic groups within its ranks.

Until the early 1990s, the Ethiopian Pentecostal movement was a recent niche phenomenon. It was not until 1967 that the *Full Gospel Believers' Church,* the first Pentecostal church in Ethiopia, was founded by students who had come into contact with the worldwide Pentecostal movement through Finnish and Swedish missionaries and American writings. In the traditionalism of late imperial Ethiopia, however, there was no room for an indigenous church outside of Orthodoxy and Western mission. An application for registration as a religious community was rejected, the students were banned from assembling, and when they protested against the unlawful restriction of their constitutionally guaranteed freedom of faith, it came to an éclat. A public meeting called in August 1972 was stormed by the police and about 250 participants were arrested and sentenced to fines or six months in prison.

After the Ethiopian revolution of 1974, Pentecostals enjoyed a few years of religious freedom. But in the course of the "Red Terror" and the increasing regulation of the Orthodox Church by the Marxist military regime, Pentecostals were again targeted by the state. By the end of the 1970s, almost all Pentecostal churches in the country had been closed, their buildings confiscated and missionaries expelled from the country. Pastors were arrested, some of them tortured and imprisoned for many years. Other Protestant denominations also came under pressure and had to close their churches completely or partially. The general secretary of the Mekane Yesus Church, Gudina Tumsa, was even kidnapped and murdered. Robust underground structures now emerged in all churches, whereby ecumenical cooperation between the clandestine churches remained the exception due to security concerns. In the state terminology, all banned Christians were considered to be "P'ent'ay", a rebellious and "counter-revolutionary" religious community.

It was not until the change of regime in 1991 that freedom of religion was granted. Underground Pentecostal churches had grown strongly and were now officially recognised. Churches were founded all over the country, also in areas with an Orthodox majority, so that conflicts were inevitable. The charismatisation of the established Protestant churches now began in earnest, mostly driven by young people. In addition, the "P'ent'ay" broke up rapidly: dozens of new denominations, hundreds of small churches and "ministries" emerged. In the course of this diversification, → prosperity theology, new doctrines, "dominion theology" (see chapter 4.4) as well as dubious prophets have gained great popularity, although the larger denominations stick to the classical formulation of Pentecostal doctrines.

After years of marginalisation, Pentecostalism has entered the mainstream in Ethiopia, and this has also found expression in organised politics. Both the last and the current prime minister of the country are Pentecostals, but the two could hardly differ more from each other. Hailemariam Desalegn, who resigned in 2018, belonged to the *Apostolic Church of Ethiopia*, a Oneness Church which rejects the doctrine of the Trinity and is therefore shunned by all other churches in Ethiopia. Abiy Ahmed, who came to power in the course of civil rights protests, is quite different and surrounded himself from the outset with the nimbus of a reformer chosen by God. Many of his political appearances are accompanied by religious rhetoric that is Pentecostal in style but expanded to include Orthodoxy, Islam and traditional practices. Abiy is thus an expression of an increasing Pentecostalisation of Ethiopian politics, but it is still uncertain what this means. His pro-democracy reconciliation and peace policies have made him a beacon of international hope in a very short time, but his increasingly opaque leadership style in face of the still unresolved crises in the country and the indefinitely postponed parliamentary elections unfortunately make it seem just as likely that the first Pentecostal politician to be honoured with the Nobel Peace Prize will follow the well-trodden paths of Ethiopian autocrats.

4.3 Exercising political responsibility

The example of some African Pentecostal churches shown here can be seen in other contexts of global Christianity as well. One can well say that the beginnings of a "Reformation movement" among Pentecostal churches are recognisable here. This is especially true since the younger generations are showing a growing interest in education and in the professionalisation of the social work of Pentecostal congregations. In the meantime, a significant number of the younger Pentecostal theologians in Africa, Asia and Latin America, even though still a minority, have received degrees or pursued doctoral studies at colleges and universities of the historically established churches.

A new tendency towards socially critical biblical hermeneutics and contextual biblical exegesis is helpful in opening up a broader theological, ethical and ecumenical discourse. This is certainly also the result of a clearly visible competition between the individual Pentecostal churches, which can only hold their own and prevail in the long term on the general religious market if they are successful in the areas of education and upward social mobility and can ensure a real improvement in the life circumstances of their members. There is also increasing pressure from political authorities and civil society that they rid themselves of scandals and excesses of abuse by certain leaders within the churches. This also helps to further learning processes within the Pentecostal church spectrum that may be compared to those of the Reformation period.

With regard to development policies, it is impressive that some Pentecostal churches are striving for a conceptual and theological dialogue with Christian development agencies, because many of them have meanwhile recognised the need to professionalise the work, reflect more thoroughly on social ethics and development theology and form stronger ecumenical networks. This generation of younger, often solidly educated and independent Pentecostal elites should not be disregarded as dialogue partners or even ignored by Christian churches and aid organisations in Western contexts. There are good opportunities here for dialogue and promising joint learning partnerships.

4.4 A political theology script: Dominion theology

Unnoticed by many contemporary observers who are occupied with the socio-political relevance of the global Pentecostal movement, a Pentecostal political theology has established itself in their churches, especially among neo-Pentecostals. This approach is the so-called "Dominionism" or "Theology of Lordship". This theology circulates in the global networks of the worldwide Pentecostal movement, reaching into the various contexts, and can therefore certainly be regarded as forming a genre intended to substantiate a Pentecostal claim to social transformation. It is promoted especially in the networks of → megachurches. The "theology of lordship" which is most obvious at present is the particular Pentecostal variant of dominion theology that has emerged and been developed in socio-politically conservative circles of Reformed theology in the United States.

The guiding principle is the concept of a "Christian reconstruction"[36] of society, in which society is divided into different social "spheres" such as family, law or economy. This model of spheres of dominion is based on the theory that modern society is decaying, and envisages a reorganisation of social life according to so-called "biblical "laws" in order ultimately to implement an authoritarian agenda and orient society towards theocratic principles. In German-language theology, similarly conservative social doctrines have been associated with the term "orders of creation" down to the recent past. The resulting problems are similar in both cases.

At the beginning of the 21st century, dominion theology was taken up and repositioned in the Pentecostal megachurch spectrum, while striving to deny any continuity with its Calvinist predecessor. Pentecostal theologians distanced themselves from any theocratic conception and thus popularised the idea of social change according to dominion theology. In doing so, the Pentecostal

---

36 This approach, which goes back to the Reformed theologian, philosopher and historian Rousas John Rushdoony (1916–2001), is also known as "reconstructionism".

version of theology of lordship incorporated fundamental concepts of reconstructionism such as the concept of spheres. In the Pentecostal variation of dominion theology, the social "spheres" are also called "pillars". The basic pattern of dominion theology categorises society in "seven spheres", which usually include core areas of social organisation such as government/state, upbringing/education, family/marriage, economy/finance, media, art/entertainment/sport and religion/church. The principal message of the theology of lordship is the transformation or reconstruction of all these social spheres. The intention is to establish cultural hegemonies. To this end, dominion theology strives for a transfer of power, by trying to get individual representatives into top positions of the respective spheres where they can operate in the sense of basic Pentecostal megachurch convictions. Dominion theology does not so much deal with the socio-structural framework, but pursues a personalised model of social intervention. The personalism inherent in this Pentecostal "long march through the institutions" distinguishes dominion theology from theological and socio-ethical concepts in the Anglo-Saxon world, which also operate with the concept of the sphere (based on communitarian ethics, which emerged in the 1980 s as a counterpart to the political liberalism of John Rawls). The primary (or ulterior) motive of the (dominating) actors also marks the difference between Pentecostal dominion theology and the functionally differentiated social theories in the German-speaking world, which often characterise the consideration of social systems such as the spheres defined by dominion theology.

One can run through this theological strategy of lordship by taking individual spheres as examples. The basic aim of most dominionist approaches is to occupy each individual sphere with "born-again" Christians in order to influence their respective practice and discourse. It is obvious, however, that alone in the sphere of politics the transformation of entire democracies into so-called "Pentecostal republics" is in the broadest sense the result of the interaction of Pentecostal networks of dominion theology. This is demonstrated at present by the "Pentecostal" presidencies in Brazil, Australia and Ethiopia, and not least by the presidency of Donald Trump in the USA, which was precisely supported by loyal Pentecostal/Charismatic milieus. This brief summary of current political processes shows that the approach of dominion theology is now accepted widely in the global Pentecostal movement, circulated in networks and contextually adapted.

⊙ Case study: Universal Church of the Kingdom of God (Igreja Universal do Reino de Deus)

One of the largest Pentecostal churches worldwide is the Universal Church of the Kingdom of God – *Igreja Universal do Reino de Deus* (IURD). This church of Brazilian origin, which resembles a globally networked company, is a classic example of a neo-Pentecostal church. In Germany, the IURD has founded permanent congregations in Berlin, Munich, Dortmund, Cologne, Frankfurt am Main, Nuremberg, Aschaffenburg, Bremen, Karlsruhe, Stuttgart and Hamburg under the title "Universal Church" or "Help Centre". The IURD is active in 83 countries worldwide.

Every day, several services are held which, according to the day of the week, are dedicated to a specific life topic. These topics are the same all over the world. On Mondays, the title "The Nation of the 318" indicates the topic of financial success. The number 318 alludes to Genesis 14:14 where Abraham chooses 318 strong warriors to save Lot. The congregation is called to consider how to be one of the 318 men who will win the battle in the world. Tuesday is dedicated to the healing of sickness and demonic possession under the heading "The Movement of the 70". The biblical background is the sending of the 70 disciples to heal and cast out demons. On Wednesdays, the "School of Intelligent Faith" is held, where you can learn how to use your faith wisely to belong to the winners in life. Thursday is about a life of partnership in marriage. On Friday, the topic of liberation is on the programme. All that deprives people of freedom is driven out and defeated: drugs, demons and other forces of darkness. On Saturday, the focus is on fasting, because renunciation means victory. Sunday is about reconciliation with God and the longing to be close to him. Spiritual renewal and participation in the fullness of life are promised. The IURD addresses life topics that speak directly to people's everyday lives. The promise of victory, success and healing in the lives of those who take part in the meetings makes the IURD highly attractive.

The first IURD church was opened in Rio de Janeiro in 1977 by Edir Macedo. He soon took on the position as bishop of the church, which already numbered 356 congregations in 1987. The estimates of the current number of members worldwide vary between six and eight million. Macedo, who had been taunted as a boy because of his handicap, has since become an icon. In 2019, the film about his life was released under the title "Nothing to lose", in which Macedo is portrayed as a man "like you and me" who experienced a touching conversion story from lottery salesman to evangelist. In 2009, Brazilian prosecutors accused Macedo of embezzling donations. His personal wealth was and is proverbial.

But the IURD as an organisation also has immense resources, which are used, among other things, to dominate public opinion through countless radio channels and major TV stations. In Brazil, the IURD is also active on the political stage. Twelve of the deputies who have joined together to represent the interests of Protestant members of the Brazilian parliament belong to the IURD. Together with the other members of this so-called *Bancada Evangélica,* they advocate, among other things, strict legislation against abortion and homosexuality.

IURD's theology advocates a conservative ethos of marriage and family. Women and girls have their own section in IURD, Godlywood. Countering the liberal moral of Hollywood, values of subordination and service in the family are made attractive to women at Godlywood. Motivated by sermons and conjured up in IURD meetings, people feel justified and empowered to attack homosexuals and transgender people both verbally and physically.

People of other faiths – especially those of Afro-Brazilian traditions – are also subject to such attacks, because preachers of the IURD see the source of power for demons and evil spirits in the ancient cults of Afro-Brazilians, which invoke and worship the spirits. The IURD followers are convinced that the stronger the strict and radical adherence to the IURD, the greater the immunity from demonic influence. They understand it as a spiritual crusade against other religions, which not infrequently turns violent.

Ultimately, the theology of the IURD follows a simple pattern of "do ut des". Believers donate at least one tenth of their income and possessions, and they are sure of God's blessings in return. This provides the IURD with a very comfortable income. Of course, in this system, there must also be proof of the fulfilment of the great promises and pledges. Therefore healing miracles are staged at most of the assemblies and exorcisms are successfully performed. People who have been healed previously also witness to the lasting benefits of the healing miracles.

The church premises of the IURD are representative and overwhelming. In Rio de Janeiro, the "World Cathedral of Faith" was built in 1999, seating 11,000 people. In 2014, a gigantic assembly hall was erected in São Paulo as a replica of the Temple of Solomon.

4.5 Aspects of ritual practice in dominion theology

Dominion theology is not limited to a socio-political concept – although this is what it claims to be. The ritual practice connected with it is essential in order to understand this Pentecostal political theology. This is made particularly clear in the understanding of "prayer", which goes hand in hand with "*spiritual warfare*", conceived as the dynamic extension of the sphere of goodness/divinity at the expense of the sphere of evil/demonism. Furthermore, the ritual practice includes the building of networks, which are spiritualised, as it were, in the megachurches. A few remarks on this:

a) Prayer

The decisive tendency towards the transformation of spheres of society leads to a change in the grammar of Pentecostal prayer.

Pentecostalism is discovering innovative social prayer practices that are at the forefront of its further politicisation. Charismatic church leaders frequently claim to have a visionary power of imagination which moves them to invent new forms of ritual. After these have been introduced in their own church, they are quickly copied or used in a modified form by other churches. One such innovation is the tradition of so-called "strategic prayer". In principle, this means an appellative form of prayer that literally commands God's intervention. It is based on the understanding that faith is a kind of contract by which God and humans enter into a bond, so that human faith can or does exert an immediate effect on divine action. Strategic prayer has unleashed a whole economy of prayer, which is intended to strengthen the ritual practice of *spiritual warfare* in the sense of dominion theology. Strategic prayer is often differentiated with regard to different levels of political action, for example between *parliamentary*, *governmental* or *harvest* prayers, relating to the hoped-for – or rather proactively implored – results of political decisions. These various forms of prayer are put into practice in correspondingly dynamic services; the worship space is run through in a prayerful manner; the body language of the praying people is energetic – after all, it is a matter of spiritual warfare. These various forms of prayer are used in correspondingly dynamic services; the congregation moves around in the church in an attitude of prayer; their body language is energetic, because they are engaged in a spiritual war; their attitude is uncompromising, not least acoustically: the prayers are considered effective when repeated at the top of one's voice – trumpeted out, as it were. The strategic prayer indicates a balancing act, trying to tip the permanent conflict between good and evil in favour of the concrete hope of the kingdom of God in the here and now. Significantly, the implied differentiation of political levels of action makes it recognisable that the goal is political influence.

⊙ **Case study: Evangelical Church of the Lutheran Confession in Brazil**

The Evangelical Church of the Lutheran Confession in Brazil (*Igreja Evangélica de Confissão Luterana no Brasil – IECLB*), a partner church of the EKD and many of the EKD's member churches and mission agencies, is particularly challenged by the presence and growth of Pentecostal churches in its country. Pastor Prof. Dr. Claudete Beise Ulrich describes the challenges for theology, counselling and church affairs which the IECLB faces in view of the aggressive attitude and expansion strategies of many Pentecostal churches. This situation is not unique to the IECLB in the context of increasing charismatisation in Brazil. What Dr. Claudete Beise Ulrich describes here is echoed in many accounts from historic Protestant churches in the countries of the Global South:

"The IECLB first encountered the Pentecostal movement in the 1960 s and saw it as an impulse for renewal and for strengthening a living spirituality. Within the IECLB, the 'Movimento Encontrão' (Fellowship movement) came into being. Reminiscent of German Pietism, the focus was on individual conversion and spiritual renewal. The aim was to reach people outside our classical Lutheran and German-born core membership, calling them to discipleship and inspiring them for the faith.

At the beginning of the 2000s, more and more pastors of the IECLB joined the charismatic movement. They began to become estranged from their church members and the IECLB. They abandoned liturgical traditions, removed religious symbols from the altars and refused to wear gowns during the service. They argued that tradition hindered the work of the Holy Spirit. The previous understanding of the sacraments was also rejected.

Children were no longer baptised. In some congregations, they introduced rebaptism. Three points in particular led to the discord between the IECLB and charismatics: the (re-)baptism of adults, the so-called spiritual warfare (believers against unbelievers) and the abolition of the Lutheran liturgy. Some congregations have left the IECLB and now call themselves 'Free Lutheran Congregation', following the tradition and theology of Pentecostal or neo-Pentecostal groups. Others continue to be in permanent conflict with large parts of the IECLB.

The IECLB has decided on a clear position, proclaiming the gospel of Jesus Christ and a life in abundance for all. This is rooted in respect for religious diversity, in the defence of human rights and a democratic society organised according to the rule of law, and in the concept of a neutral state in which all people are respected and their dignity is upheld – also in face of attacks from fundamentalist Pentecostals and neo-Pentecostals.

Many Pentecostals reject a theology that reaches out to the poor. They prefer to declare that people are themselves to blame for their poverty. Recently, a pastor of the IECLB mentioned in the intercessions the problems of state school teachers and the need for pension reform. As a result, she was strongly criticised for making political statements at the altar.

Because of the fundamentalist Pentecostals, the IECLB is challenged to adhere uncompromisingly to denominational principles. These include the historical-critical interpretation of the Holy Scriptures and the Lutheran confessions, the understanding of the Bible as the Word of God recorded by humans, the confession of the historical Christ who was crucified and resurrected, and the responsibility for the preservation of creation. The Bible may not be used as an instrument of power by evangelical Pentecostals.

The IECLB wants to expose the commercialisation of faith, as Martin Luther did in his time. It opposes the selling of salvation, as does the Lutheran World Federation under the motto "Salvation not for Sale". The longing for salvation must not be abused by false promises and the sale of accessories or blessings. The IECLB has an important theological contribution to offer, as a Protestant church, by holding on to the fact that the gospel of Jesus Christ has ethical implications. If the IECLB takes leave of this principle in order to compete in the religious market and retain its members, it will lose its identity as the Church of Jesus Christ in Brazil.

Some evangelisation campaigns in Latin America support the appropriation of land by revival Christians at the expense of the indigenous population. They also contribute to the massive persecution of the Afro-Brazilian population by spreading prejudices on demonisation. In this way, religion is misused to illegally appropriate land, oppress the people and exploit the cultural and natural wealth of the country.

I would like to recall the phenomenon of Christofascism, a term coined by Dorothee Sölle*. Christofascism means that religion and politics are so intertwined that the use of weapons and violence is justified in the name of Jesus Christ. Sölle describes three basic features of Christofascism: the fusion of Christian theology with capitalist ideology and nationalism, a rigorous work ethic and a reassertion of traditional images of the family that assign a subordinate role to women. In this Christofascist system, freedom of the press is restricted by censorship. National security is invoked as a sacred doctrine. Issues of solidarity and justice are systematically suppressed. This is exactly the phenomenon we are currently experiencing in Brazilian society.

Theologically, a God of glory (Deus gloriae) is proclaimed in the many Pentecostal and neo-Pentecostal churches. Luther, on the other hand, placed the crucified God at the midpoint. The power of God is shown in weakness and not in the power of arms – that is the message of the gospel." (Claudete Beise Ulrich)

* *Dorothee Sölle,* The Window of Vulnerability: A Political Spirituality, 1990, Augsburg Fortress Publishing.

A theological comparison with other megachurch approaches is worthwhile. There, the visionary immediacy to God is often elaborated in the style of sensational journalism. The subject is encountered in the supranatural sphere, but politics is not in the sights of spiritual warfare. Nonetheless, battle prayers remain part of ritual practice. This ritual practice is also cultivated in the daughter congregations of → megachurches in Germany, for example. This does not apply universally to all megachurch offshoots. The battle prayer practice is particularly prominent in those congregations that go back to the so-called "Fire" ministries (mostly of Nigerian origin), whose very name explicitly refers to the ritual "cleansing" of the individual from demonic powers and influences. The reference to social issues, on the other hand, is secondary. The ritual practice of battle prayers is far less prominent in those megachurch local congregations focusing, for example, on church growth. It is even less to be found in Pentecostal congregations that have arisen locally in Germany or that have abandoned this practice and broken away from the megachurches.[37]

---

37 Thus the results of the comparative study *Andreas Heuser/Claudia Hoffmann*, Afrikanische Migrationskirchen und ihre selektive ökumenische Konnektivität, in: Pastoraltheologie 107, 2018, 293–306.

b) Visionary genealogies and horizontal networks

Megachurch networking as well as the constant concentration of networks are an integral part of the theology of lordship. A distinction can be made between vertical networks, which develop within a church, and horizontal networks, which are cultivated between individual churches and groups of people. Such networks have developed, for example, within the US American "apostolic and prophetic" vanguard of an independent megachurch sector of the Pentecostal movement. In Brazil, this corresponds to the parliamentary group *Bancada Evangélica*, in which deputies of different parties, including many representatives of Pentecostal churches, have joined together to implement evangelical values in politics. The network structure includes targeted cooperation between highly influential charismatic individuals. Since their explicit principal goals are to transform society as a whole, classical orientations towards church planting or strategies for congregational growth recede into the background. The main actors of this relational (non-institutional) "apostolic network building" strive to bundle concepts as well as resources through mutual exchange, especially at conferences. They attach importance to the horizontal channels by which the vanguard of the so-called "apostolic revolution" legitimises itself mutually and publicly confirms the apostolic-prophetic authority that it claims for itself. The network creates a profile for the charismatic leader whose innovative power is supposed to unfold limitlessly in the exercise of direct, God-given authority. In the meantime, the cooperation extends across national boundaries, for example between Afro-American and African megachurches.

The enormous network of megachurches, which has long been active on a global scale, is knit together by a "visionary genealogy". This implies that the charismatic personality is formed through mutual reinforcement. The confirmation of visionary charism depends crucially on the involvement in recognised prophetic networks. These networks can also include formations of apostolic groups, so that in the global Pentecostal movement and at regional levels several such networks can work together and support one another at the same time. The social construction of the megachurch charisms hinders both isolated, individual positions and personal monopolisation of charismatic authority.

Within these various possibilities of networking, arrangements for succession are also authenticated; the visionary genealogy regulates, as it were, the apostolic successions within the networks. The network architecture here provides for very significant forms of ritual incorporation known as apostolic covering and transferable anointing, or impartation of power. The power of the Holy Spirit is to be passed on, or the visionary-prophetic gift in a megachurch circle reinforced, through acts of anointing. Those who find access to such a network enhance the profile of their own church. Lesser known "apostles" and "prophets" can position themselves close to the recognised megachurch augurs. Access to such a network node is usually linked to years of proven loyalty. Ambitious megachurch leaders who wish to gain positions within the network are also required to make significant financial investments. They have to convene conferences and → crusades (urban mass evangelisations), to organise the expansion of their own churches and the training of full-time and voluntary workers, to present themselves at international meetings or to invite high-profile guest preachers to their own events. At the same time, existing networks are constantly being revitalised and expanded through new relational constellations.

4.6 International networks and questions of political ethics in an ecumenical context

The Evangelische Kirche in Deutschland (EKD) and its ministries have been connected to the ecumenical movement and committed to its goals from the very beginning. The relations between the WCC and the Pentecostal churches are therefore also important for the EKD and its member churches and a possible point of orientation when it comes to new relations or partner dialogues. In the WCC, one can distinguish between the following groups of relations with Pentecostal and independent churches, characterised by differing degrees of closeness and commitment:

a) Although in the first three decades the vast majority of Pentecostal churches were anti-ecumenical, there were also Pentecostal churches that were open to ecumenical cooperation and dialogue. As early as 1961, the first Pentecostal churches were admitted as official member churches of the WCC (among them two Chilean churches *Iglesia Pentecostal de Chile* and the *Missión Iglesia Pentecostal*, later the *Igreja Evangélica Pentecostal "O Brasil para Cristo"* [Manoel de Mello] from Brazil, and then since 1972 the *International Evangelical Church and Missionary Association*). Today, the WCC has seven Pentecostal member churches, not counting the → African Instituted Churches (AIC), which are also Pentecostal. Some of these African independent churches are also full members of the WCC (e. g. *Church of the Lord Aladura*, Nigeria); the Organization of African Instituted Churches (OAIC) is an associate member of the All African Conference of Churches (AACC) and works closely with the WCC.

b) A large number of Pentecostal churches that are not connected to the WCC as such are nevertheless members of its re-

gional or national equivalents, i.e. national councils of churches. There they cooperate with other historical churches. For
example, Evangelical, Independent and Pentecostal churches
are members of all 16 national councils of churches on the African continent. Some of them are currently being supported in
Africa by *Brot für die Welt* and thus – through this ecumenical
connection – already belong indirectly to the partners of this
development aid agency.

c) Since 1965 there has also been a working relationship between the WCC and some Pentecostal churches which are
non-members. Certain representatives of Pentecostal churches have participated in all WCC Assemblies since 1968, have
been called to serve on the Faith and Order Commission and
to participate in the Commission on World Mission and Evangelism. At the 1991 Assembly in Canberra, member churches
were called upon to acknowledge congregations of Pentecostal
churches as "part of the historical development of the Christian
churches and their rich diversity", to contribute to the promotion of relations with Pentecostal churches and to intensify the
critical dialogue between Pentecostal churches that are open to
the ecumenical movement with Pentecostal churches that are
critical towards it.

d) Reference has already been made to the important role of
the → Global Christian Forum (GCF), which sees itself as an extended ecumenical platform and is particularly concerned with
involving the Pentecostal movement (cf. Chapter 2.4).

The areas and structures of ecumenical cooperation of the
WCC outlined above are a necessary first minimum condition for examining the question of whether projects and

churches from the charismatic and Pentecostal spectrum can become dialogue and project partners of EKD churches or ministries. The EKD does not maintain relations with churches that are hostile or dismissive towards ecumenical cooperation.

Another difficulty is that different types of Pentecostal/ Charismatic churches send very different signals of interest with regard to ecumenical dialogue and joint learning about responsible political ethics. A rural grassroots Pentecostal church oriented towards development work and social empowerment with the poorest of the poor may be ecumenically very differently oriented from congregations of neo-Pentecostal and megachurch networks that are marked by certain forms of dominion theology and internal debates about its global implementation in regional contexts. As described above in chapter 4.4, they are guided by ideas that assume the existence of (social) spheres which they intend to occupy strategically. In this, they reveal a basic interest that is hardly ecumenical, but in part decidedly anti-ecumenical. Megachurch neo-Pentecostal networks are very flexible, as they show little interest in institutionalisation and prefer the mobility potential of relational networks. Megachurch (horizontal) networks are constantly changing through new constellations, alignments and changes of personnel or churches at their meeting points. This dynamism corresponds with the waywardness of megachurches, which existentially goes back to their founding figures. Since megachurches function autonomously, according to their own laws, they initially show no inclination for ecumenical networking outside the Pentecostal, megachurch spectrum. This is also evident with regard to so-called migration churches in Germany with a Pentecostal character. The ecumenical connectivity of migration churches with a megachurch Pentecostal background is much less pronounced than in the case of locally developed charismatic migration churches or branch congregations of African independent churches. Megachurch offshoots tend to refer to the normative model of their "headquarters" in the whole of their church and theological culture. This corresponds to the global expansion policy of megachurches (their description of "mission"), which tends to be controlled centrally and is therefore less likely to engage in local ecumenical exchange relationships.

Nevertheless, it should be noted that some of the megachurches are certainly engaging in ecumenical processes. Opening up to the ecumenical movement takes time, in which trust can develop, and experience with each other. The → Global Christian Forum (GCF) has a broker function here. One of the declared aims of the GCF is to break up the various camps in worldwide Christianity and to broaden the frame of reference of ecumenical dialogue. It aims to facilitate dialogue processes between WCC member churches and evangelical and Pentecostal churches, but also "independent churches" that are not or cannot be members of the WCC. At its second meeting, which took place in Manado, Indonesia, in 2011, the initiative to invite megachurches was the clearest up to now. For the first time, some megachurches participated in a forum meeting. The "Message from Manado" mapped out some of the pressing issues for the future of the ecumenical movement. These include, for example, the unjust distribution of resources in the world and also efforts towards interreligious dialogue. The "Message from Manado" took up a core megachurch concern by mentioning a stronger focus on church growth. However, even at the most recent meeting of the GCF, convened in Bogotá in 2018, there were regrets about the still relatively low participation of mega-churches. It remains to be seen whether this participation of megachurches in ecumenical processes will change in the foreseeable future and how this will deepen the broader ecumenical dialogue qualitatively.

In any case, there are some remarkable approaches in areas of social change that are having an increasing influence on theological discourse. At the same time, it can be seen that the Pentecostal movement is in many cases still struggling with theological concepts of social commitment, such as ecclesial social ethics, so that these could become a fruitful subject for ecumenical dialogue. In debates on the forms of political involvement of Pentecostal churches and the underlying reasons, individual Pentecostal leaders are often named, whose communicative charisma has opened the door to the centre of national government. Good relations and close contact with individual (often also Pentecostal) politicians are seen as particularly desirable. Well prepared and structured statements on social policy, developed by experts and specialists on issues of economy, education and ecology, are indeed within the scope of the dominion theology outlined above, but they have hardly come into view up to now. With this in mind, mission agencies or development organisations should review their partnership work, if necessary extending their focus beyond the training and support of members of the historical Protestant churches or secular NGOs and offering joint training to the new generation of Pentecostal leaders in the area of social and ecologically sustainable development responsibility.

4.7 World responsibility: Criteria for an ecumenical learning dialogue

The representatives of politics and foundations in church and society are increasingly confronted with the task of tightening the criteria that determine which churches come into question as contact, dialogue or even project partners, and which do not. It should be noted that the position of Protestant churches in Germany cannot be reduced to one simple formula. On the other hand, it must be ensured that the criteria for a learning dialogue with Pentecostal/Charismatic churches are compatible both with the basic obligations assumed by the EKD as a member church of the World Council of Churches and with credibility concerning the care for fundamental human rights. Partnership and openness towards Pentecostal churches may not contradict the ecumenical responsibilities of the EKD, but must correspond and adhere to them. This means

- that *dialogue and connection* can take place where there are signs in new churches of a positive desire to learn more on issues of social responsibility of the church, the concerns of development and sustainability;
- that *partnership and cooperation* can take place with those churches and fellowships that are committed to ecumenical openness and cooperation with other churches, e. g. through membership in a national council of churches or a national evangelical alliance, and that share certain common theological convictions on mission and development, as reflected for example in the statement "Christian Witness in a Multi-Religious World" (by the WCC, the Vatican and the World Evangelical Alliance), in the documents of the Micah Initiative in the evangelical field, or in recent

WCC study documents on an ecumenical understanding of mission;

■ that *demarcation and defence* have to take place immediately if and when forms of church or groups are identified that place Christian values and symbols in the service of regimes or political parties which are repressive and hostile to human rights, or that deliberately refuse ecumenical dialogue and engage in aggressive mission as well as excessive forms of spiritual abuse of power (cf. chapter 3.10).

In a fundamental decision at its Assembly in Canberra in 1991, the World Council of Churches adopted important recommendations for all member churches with regard to their relationship with Pentecostal churches (see chapter 5.4).[38] However, a further development of these recommendations in the direction of a practicable criteriology for ecumenical dialogue and partnership work, also in the sense of protecting the human rights and credibility standards of the ecumenical movement, has not yet been achieved at the level of the WCC.

In order to put these basic options for the attitude towards charismatic and Pentecostal churches into practice, there will have to be different methods according to the different levels of church activity:

---

38 These recommendations were also taken up in substance in the policy document "Common Understanding and Vision of the WCC" (CUV document) adopted at the Harare Assembly, which also decided the formation of the Global Christian Forum: "The fellowship of the WCC is limited by the absence of other churches which, for various reasons, have not sought membership. For example, unjustifiable barriers have arisen between the WCC and some Evangelical and Pentecostal churches because of tendencies on both sides to caricature or remain indifferent to each other."

For the level of a church as a whole (regional church, free church), those ecumenical criteria are decisive which also result from membership and the joint formation of an opinion with the regional Christian councils. (The opening to a further dimension of ecumenism may not call into question the ecumenical relations with other churches that have developed in the course of time.)

- ■ For a church district or a local congregation, special criteria can apply in relation to individual charismatic migration churches in the neighbourhood, paying attention to the concerns of the pastoral care of refugees and people with a migration background (practical solidarity is urgently necessary wherever tasks can be accomplished in the field of humanitarian or social work, especially in the context of migration).

- ■ For a church agency that manages funds from church tax, donations and public grants, special and stricter criteria apply that go beyond the general WCC standards and are also related to financial due diligence and accountability towards donors and third party funders.

- ■ For the activities of the church in the field of development, ecumenism and mission, coherent criteria of theology, ecumenism, development concerns and human rights are just as applicable as institutional reliability and capacity. An opening for cooperation with new churches only makes sense where it results in a functional added value for achieving the basically targeted goals, whether for development, ecumenism or ecumenical mission.[39] Likewise, a strict principle of

---

39 See also *Heinrich Wilhelm Schäfer*, Friedenspotenzial von Freikirchen in den USA und Lateinamerika. Potenziale und Hindernisse für die internationale Zusammenarbeit (ifa-Edition Kultur und Außenpolitik), Stuttgart 2019 (https://doi.org/10.17901/AKBP1.09.2019).

ecumenical reference also applies: churches of the Pentecostal/Charismatic type that are already cooperating in regional or international ecumenical structures and have been recommended by their ecumenical partners for further partnership enjoy clear priority. This means, by way of example, that the following criteria must be examined in the case of potential dialogue partners:

- willingness and openness to ecumenical dialogue with other churches or development networks,
- religious non-discrimination in outreach and access to social services and development projects,
- capacity for accountability and transparency in the use of funds,
- peace compatibility of mission and proclamation (which in the case of clearly aggressive militancy in the language and practice of proclamation can hardly be expected),
- relevant impact of rural and social development programmes,
- existence of an ecumenical or development-related regional need that cannot be met by other partners from the traditional partner field,
- potential for transformation and reinforcement of hope through the proclamation and ministry of the respective church for its target groups (this also means, for example, that one should observe with an open mind whether churches are offering empowerment or consolation).

It is important to keep in mind that the effectiveness of Pentecostal/Charismatic churches is not only a challenge for historical denominational churches, but is also often under critical observation by secular institutions (foundations) and governments in the southern hemisphere.

⊙ **Case study: "Christ for all Nations" – Missionswerk Reinhard Bonnke**

The evangelist Reinhard Bonnke (1940–2019) described himself as "God's combine harvester" and placed his work under the slogan: "Africa shall be saved!" Reinhard Willi Gottfried Bonnke was born in 1940 in Königsberg (now Kaliningrad) as the son of the pastor of a Pentecostal church. As early as 1950 he experienced the inner call to go into the mission in Africa. In 1959 he attended a Bible school in Great Britain, was ordained in 1960 and served as a pastor in the German Association of Pentecostal Churches (BFP) until 1966. From 1967 to 1974 he worked as a BFP missionary in the independent mountain state of Lesotho. He had a tent constructed there for 800 people, later for 10,000, but it could soon no longer accommodate the crowds at his crusades. He extended his activities into other countries. "Fire Conferences" were held parallel to the crusades in order to train pastors and other staff. In 1974, Bonnke moved to Witfield, a suburb of Johannesburg, where he founded the mission organisation *"Christ for all Nations"* from 1974 to 1975, whose headquarters have been in Frankfurt am Main since 1986. There are further independent offices in Africa, the USA, Canada and England.

In 1982 Bonnke was invited to Seoul by the Korean Pentecostal church leader Yonggi Cho. In 1983 Bonnke visited the USA, where he met the Pentecostal healing evangelist Tommy Lee Osborn, who acknowledged that Bonnke was "the greater". Pat Robertson, the owner of the television station CBN, let Bonnke appear for the first time in his broadcasts. He also gained the attention of C. Peter Wagner, a "key leader" of the Church Growth Movement and co-initiator of the

"Third Wave of the Holy Spirit". Bonnke adopted Wagner's concept of *"spiritual warfare"* and the Unitarian, Trinity-critical theology that represents the charismatised evangelicalism of the *Third Wave*. After Bonnke's death in 2019, his students immediately continued his work.

Bonnke represents the type of Euro-American "salvation preachers" which are now active transnationally. The decisive factors are:

- emphasis on healing theology and its performative practice at large events,
- significance of the transcontinental space between Europe, Asia, Africa and America and how this is constituted in the Pentecostal world-wide discourse regarding missionary activities,
- connections with Independent Churches in Africa with their networks of relationships, which one can often only describe as flexible, temporary "cooperations", but not as networks designed for a longer period of time and intensity of contacts.

The "Fire Conference" of 1986 went down in the annals of Pentecostalism; it reportedly influenced thousands of African pastors and evangelists. Bonnke's ideas about the task of evangelism cannot be separated from his self-assurance in view of his success. Quotes such as this bear witness to this: "Then I saw more converts in one night than a whole African mission station in a hundred years." And in the same vein: "...but our primary concern in evangelism is effectiveness."*

Bonnke's success is not least due to the fact that he succeeds in harmonising the traditional African understanding of reality with biblical anthropology and cosmology and in appropriating it himself. In his evangelistic preaching, he presents the way to escape from the dilemmas of guilt, witchcraft, fear of spirits and demons, illness, curses and persecution and also from flagrant violence, corruption and poverty. His cooperation with other preachers was decisive, whether from the local area or prominent in Africa. Bonnke's alleged healings, going as far as raising the dead, with which he purported to be able to fulfil the expectations of people in their hopeless situations, must be viewed critically. In 2001, during a campaign in northern Nigeria, riots broke out between Christians and Muslims, resulting in the deaths of hundreds of people. In 2001, Bonnke tried to convert people to Christianity in Germany with his brochure "From Minus to Plus". This campaign was largely unsuccessful.

* *Reinhard Bonnke*, Evangelism by Fire. Igniting Your Passion for the Lost, Frankfurt a.M. 1999, 27, and idem "... Time is Running Out. Save the world – before it's too late", Ventura, CA 1999, 103. Cf. also the analysis of Bonnke's personality in *Kürschner-Pelkmann* 2004, 41.

4.8 State intervention, taking the example of South Africa

A particularly interesting example is a process in South Africa by which the preaching and financial behaviour of some churches and religious communities were more closely investigated on the initiative of the South African government. The focus was not only on Pentecostal churches, but on all religious groups. From 2016 to 2017 there was a working and dialogue project combined with a survey. An official government commission had identified in some of the Pentecostal and other churches and religious communities a series of increasingly irritating extreme events[40] and objectionable practices which had been publicised. This was taken as an opportunity for the government to raise the question of common standards and new regulations. The South African government set up the *Cultural, Religious and Linguistic Communities (CRL) Rights Commission.* The CRL commission is an independent body of experts which, according to its statutes, can investigate issues of religious integrity, conflicts between majorities and minorities, as well as standards of religious practice and financial management, and therefore has a considerable range of legal powers, including the subpoena of religious leaders. In the course of 2016 and 2017, the CRL commission, based on a series of regional hearings and interviews with religious leaders, presented a comprehensive investigation on the "Commercialisation of Religion and Abuse of People's Belief Systems" in South Africa, which is an eye-opener. The 65-page final report did not examine all religious communities in South Africa on a representative basis, but only interviewed 85 religious leaders selected at random from very different religious traditions. The aim of the qualitative interviews was nevertheless linked to ambitious goals, which were expressed in a series of key questions:

- How can we better understand the phenomenon and the causes for the commercialisation of religion and healing?
- What deep convictions make people in our country vulnerable to the messages that emanate from such religious ceremonies?

---

40 See, inter alia, the report recorded in the Commission: "A South African preacher made his congregation eat grass to 'be closer to God' before stamping on them. Under the instruction of a certain pastor, dozens of his followers dropped to the floor to eat the grass at his church after being told it would 'bring them closer to God'. These methods have drawn criticism from thousands of people although members of his congregation swear by his method – he is said to have claimed that human beings can eat anything to feed their bodies and survive whatever they choose to eat."

- How do we assess the religious framework and its relevance to deal with the prevailing religious challenges?
- What findings and recommendations address the status quo on commercialized religion and healing?
- Why are religious institutions spreading so much in our country?
- What various miraculous claims are made by religious leaders and traditional healers regarding the powers to heal and make miracles?
- What form of legal framework can regulate the religious sectors?

The final report of the state enquiry highlighted a number of questionable examples of church misconduct and what it described as religious manipulation, especially in the area of neo-Pentecostal and megachurches externally controlled from outside South Africa. These include, among others

- organisational and administrative deficiencies in a number of religious organisations. This includes failure to register as non-profit-organisations (NPOs) and maintaining of financial records;
- deliberate exploitation of poor and vulnerable people through assumption of divine/missionary right to solicit fees for healing and receive tithes in cash or in kind from their members without commitment to responsible financial management and accounting;
- inspiring deification and hero-worship of church leaders by members of their churches ("personality cult"), making them immune from all kinds of critical questioning or accountability;
- cases of psychological repression of members of religious communities, in some cases preventing proper medical

treatment and replacing medical control with healing rituals;

- failing to mark the boundaries between registering as private commercial companies and registering as religious communities.

The summary of the CRL commission's findings reads like a disturbing panorama of certain excessive religious practices and practices of abuse of spiritual power; it indicates serious deficiencies in the common self-regulation of religious communities within a social context of high vulnerability and low social protection. Deficits with regard to the prevention of religious extremism and religious abuse have been uncovered and important questions are raised with regard to more quality control and common minimum training standards, which should be linked to the questions of admission to a spiritual pastoral ministry.

4.9 Political abuse of religion: Ecumenical dissociation

The experiences of Southern Africa, but also examples in the Latin American context, show that there are certain Pentecostal churches which have had – or used – little opportunity to participate in dialogue with other churches, or which for years have either refused any ecumenical dialogue or felt excluded from it. These churches sometimes play a fatal political role and can cause massive losses of credibility for Christianity as a whole. Traditional denominational churches, as well as Pentecostal and independent churches willing to engage in dialogue, must therefore be strengthened and encouraged to overcome misguided forms of proclamation, development concepts and pastoral practice, to practise self-criticism on matters of the church, theology and politics, and to develop instruments for a critical social-ethical tradition in their respective context. This is now also seen in part within Pentecostal circles. The experience with the South African governmental commission and its report on the commercialisation of religion and the exploitation of traditional beliefs from 2016/2017 shows that churches and aid agencies must and can take the task of theological self-criticism and self-correction of the different types of Christian churches more seriously. It is remarkable that ecumenical organisations such as the All Africa Conference of Churches (AACC), the WCC or even important Latin American churches have made the critical dialogue with the Charismatic-Pentecostal movement an organic part of their future phase of work or strategy of action. In the discussion on "Misleading Theologies" (AACC symposium in Nairobi in November 2019), core elements of distortions of Christian theology were clearly elaborated in three thematic areas (prosperity and holistic development; health and healing; power and authority).[41] The question is how such impulses for the churches' self-correction can be further publicised regionally on a larger scale and also supported by ecumenical partners.

4.10 Considerations for gaining competence in development and sustainability

The core problem characterising the controversial debate on the recommendations of the South African CRL commission indeed

---

41 Cf. the recent publication of the AACC in view of various forms of spiritual abuse of power with misleading forms of theology in African Christianity: https://www.oikoumene.org/news/african-ecumenical-group-releases-book-on-misleading-theologies.

points to an internal problem of the increasing differentiation in the religious landscape and religious communities, which is not only a South African phenomenon. Personal reports from charismatic-Pentecostal churches heighten the impression that the key to better quality control and prevention of abuse and extremism lies with those representatives of charismatic *and* traditional denominational churches who are capable of dialogue and can be a *common* concern of both. Over and above the necessary procedures of registering religious communities as non-profit organisations (NPOs) and of quality assurance in the field of religious operations, it is specially important to address the question of common training and further education of church leaders and religious functionaries. How can the positive interest and the increasing openness for dialogue and joint leadership training be channelled into common, widely effective programmes in order to achieve not only better qualification, but also quality assurance for preaching and social service as well as defence against religious abuse? Can ecumenical partners contribute to the development and promotion of a joint initiative at regional level for a pilot programme over several years to train representatives of Pentecostal churches and leaders of traditional denominational churches in the areas of politically responsible ethics, sustainable development and orderly church leadership?

The consequence for ecumenical dialogue in Germany, in particular between German Protestant churches and Pentecostal congregations, is that questions of political responsibility for the world, of a common responsibility for an ethic of peace, justice and sustainability cannot be sidelined at ecumenical encounters. Rather, it is important to create a context in which difficult and controversial issues can also be discussed, allowing the respective dialogue partners to pose – and respond to – critical and open theological and ethical questions. To this end, Chapter 5 will now formulate suggestions on how insights and theological reflections, exemplary cases and ecumenical approaches can be made fruitful for encounters at various levels.

5. Practical recommendations for ecumenical relations with Pentecostal churches and the charismatic movement

With the Charta Oecumenica (2001), the churches in Europe committed themselves to bear witness together to the love and hope for all people, in word and deed and the power of the Holy Spirit. In diverse forms of ecumenical cooperation and ecumenical dialogue, they want to take steps towards unity, reconciliation and an ever more intensive fellowship. This includes not taking divisions for granted in the awareness of one's own guilt, but working towards overcoming them, treating still painful wounds of the past by the "healing of memories", and praying for and with each other for Christian unity. Furthermore, it is important to work towards an understanding of the contents and goals of the social responsibility of Christians and towards a common commitment to peace and reconciliation of cultures and religions, justice and the integrity of creation. In this chapter it will be shown how ecumenical orientation can find appropriate expression and lead to visible change in the practice of congregations (5.2), at the level of church leadership (5.3), in the project work and development cooperation of the churches (5.4) and in theological education (5.5). This is preceded by a review of the initial criteria (5.1).

5.1 Initial criteria for the ecumenical journey

A central role in the process of ecumenical encounter and rapprochement is played by the national "Council of Christian

Churches in Germany" (ACK). The ACK has been establishing relations with charismatic groups and Pentecostal churches at local, regional and national level since the 1960s. The → Mülheim Association is a member, and the → Association of Pentecostal Churches (BFP) a guest member of ACK Germany. At the regional church level, Pentecostal-charismatic churches and international congregations with a Pentecostal background often have the status of observers or guests. At the local level, Pentecostal congregations sometimes also participate as full members. However, it can be observed that Pentecostal neighbours often have reservations about participating in the ACK. On the other hand, it should be noted that the acceptance of Pentecostal congregations as full members at the local ACK level can be relevant for being admitted to membership on the next higher level, so that it is absolutely necessary to conduct an honest examination of the substance of the common ecumenical path at this level.

Among the continuing obstacles to dialogue are a negative image of ecumenism and the traditional denominations on the part of some spokespersons for the Pentecostal churches, and a strongly prevailing attitude of rejection and disqualification of Pentecostal congregations and charismatic movements in wide circles of the other churches – sometimes still designating them as "sects".

At its Assembly in Canberra in 1991, the World Council of Churches formulated recommendations for ecumenical dialogue with Pentecostal and charismatic brothers and sisters in faith in the document "The Unity of the Church as Koinonia: Gift and Calling". The principles laid down there are guiding for all member churches of the WCC and therefore also determine the attitude within the EKD towards Pentecostal and charismatic churches and congregations.

Sensitive behaviour and mutual approach to one another also imply the recollection of injuries and guilt. In the past, the historical churches in Germany have repeatedly looked at Pentecostal churches and charismatic movements with theological arrogance and hurtful apologia, nurturing stereotypes of otherness. Recognising guiding interests and misjudgments on both sides is an important step towards more truthfulness and truth, towards the "healing of memories", towards sustainable reconciliation and living fellowship. Ecumenical dialogue challenges all those involved to reflect anew on their own theological perspectives, to question stereotypical perceptions, to be inspired by forms of living spirituality and to allow themselves to be surprised and sometimes criticised in ecumenical encounters; where necessary, they should also question the perspectives of the other side and take a critical stand. One must be attentively aware of internal differences within the Pentecostal movement, especially when the dialogue with the ecumenical partner touches on controversial issues. A discernment of spirits can help ecumenical dialogue partners to distance themselves from problematic developments in their own ranks. This includes questionable theological positions as well as organisational forms and leadership styles which, for example, enable spiritual abuse of power. Such mutual interaction presupposes a trusting dialogue tradition which has to be established. The following perspectives can provide guidance on the common path:

- The ecumenical dialogue with Pentecostal churches and with charismatic congregations encourages the rediscovery of the gift of the Holy Spirit in the New Testament, the development of one's own theology of the Holy Spirit and a stronger focus on the effect of the Holy Spirit in believers' lives.

■ It is recognised that congregations of Pentecostal churches form part of the historical development of Christian churches and their rich diversity.

■ Dialogue is sought with the Pentecostal churches and lively relationships are cultivated.

■ The WCC encourages study projects that promote the knowledge of diversity in Pentecostalism.

These basic options contain different possibilities for the development of ecumenical dialogue and cooperation on the different levels of church activity, which will be explained in the following sections:

■ Getting to know and understanding each other,

■ Implementing ecumenical dialogues and understanding at the leadership level,

■ Ecumenical orientation towards joint world responsibility and worldwide project work,

■ Anchoring ecumenism in theology and theological education.

5.2 Getting to know and understanding each other – at the local level

Identifying places

Pentecostal and charismatic congregations are not necessarily recognisable by their church steeple. Many congregations hold their services and Bible studies in offices, multi-purpose rooms or on former industrial premises. In particular, international Pentecostal charismatic congregations often rent rooms from other congregations and hold their services when the local Lutheran, Reformed, Baptist, Methodist or Adventist congregation does not need them. There are other congregations that change their venues constantly – either because they cannot afford to rent a place for a longer period, or because it is part of their concept to rent new rooms spontaneously according to the growth of the congregation and to make the respective meeting place known via social media. For a Pentecostal charismatic congregation, changing addresses is either pragmatic or born out of need or other necessities. Venues and structures follow people and their mobility much more closely than in traditional congregations.

Using and strengthening Christian councils

The local Council of Christian Churches (ACK) can be a helpful partner when searching for Pentecostal Christians in the neighbourhood, but it can also have an invigorating and inspiring effect on some local ACKs when Christians from member churches do not stop at the existing ecumenical horizon and encourage the ACK to join them in the search for new neighbours.

Tracking down border-crossers

When exploring ecumenical neighbourhoods one has to bid farewell to clear templates and unambiguous classifications. Firstly, there are groups in many churches and congregations whose piety and prayer life do not differ greatly from charismatic forms. These can be groups from the pietist fellowships in the regional Protestant church, members of the local church with a migratory background, people who feel connected to a certain style of Christian music, or mission-oriented youth groups. Taking account of these and other groups on the margins of the mainstream congregation and inviting them into the search as bridge builders can lead to transformation and reconciliation in a congregation. Secondly, there are always members of one congregation who are in contact with Christians and groups from other congregations and sometimes also attend their services. It is true that people in Germany are much less flexible in their allegiance to a particular church than is the case in other countries such as the USA and many countries of the Global South. But here in Germany, too, there is now a market of churches, religions and religious offerings which even members of traditional churches do not necessarily ignore. When looking for charismatic neighbours, one has the chance to appreciate these border-crossers, upon whom the official church often only disdainfully smiles, as innovative and unconventional people and to understand their motives for an open Christian identity as a valuable part of ecumenical dialogue.

Making visits

"You visited me" (Mt 25:36). Visiting is a basic Christian virtue, not just an act of mercy, even though that is the focus of Matthew 25. Visiting means building fellowship and strengthening it. Visiting and hospitality are two sides of the same coin. Visits between congregations in different places and of different character have shaped the life of Christian congregations since apostolic times. To put oneself in another person's hands as a guest, to confide in them, to allow them to set the rules, let their culture and home form the framework – that is a virtue that is sometimes underestimated in the many discourses around hospitality.

A visit is a venture – but "nothing ventured, nothing gained" in neighbourhood relations. Church services are public events, open to all. Even better is attendance with an invitation, not a spontaneous visit, but one that is expected. If a guest or a group of guests say when they are coming, the hosts can better prepare to receive them.

Holding conversations

The individual contacts between Christians of charismatic traditions and historical denominations can help to start small discussion groups where people get to know each other better, learn something about the faith and piety of the other tradition, and ask questions. In this way, the participants are less uncertain, and it is possible to build up relationships that do not connect Christians from the other tradition with preconceptions that are often only theoretical and do not correspond to reality.

Ecumenical encounters and dialogues can also take place at courses on the Christian faith. When people are preparing for baptism or baptismal renewal, they will be reminded of the breadth and diversity of Christianity during the introductory course. However, it is most important to experience dialogue with other traditions as enriching, not threatening, even if one decides in favour of a particular denomination.

Meetings with confirmation parents can also be an opportunity to discuss experiences in families of mixed denominations, leading to ecumenical discussion. This can offer support to young people who are often seriously open at confirmation age to religious themes and spiritual experiences, as long as they see in them an authentic expression of Christian faith. The discussion with Christians from charismatic groups is particularly relevant here. The realisation that no insurmountable division exists here, but that both sides seek and wish to learn from and enrich each other, can disperse the rigid "either/or" of denominational commitment. Many people need a different expression of their faith in a certain life phase than in another phase. In ecumenical friendship one can accept such needs and not condemn them as "church hopping".

Bible sharing

Ecumenical and intercultural Bible sharing can also be a method by which the common foundation of the biblical text corrects the perspective towards one another. Studying the biblical text as the common source of faith can diminish the tendency to have a one-sided image of the "others". With a formalised structure, such Bible conversations leave room for the personal piety of the various participants, whilst preventing them from dominating the discussion with a particular opinion on the Bible.

Using events

Regular ecumenical appointments have long become a standard feature in many churches, such as the World Day of Prayer, the Week of Prayer for Christian Unity, the Evangelical Alliance Week of Prayer, the Day of Prayer for the Care of Creation, the Long Night of Churches, the Intercultural Week, the Peace Week, and many more. Many of these events are carefully prepared by the Council of Christian Churches in Germany, and joint ceremonies and worship services at the national level are now attended by high-ranking representatives from church and society, who take the opportunity to express their attitude towards ecumenism and peaceful coexistence. On the local level, these events can also be prepared and organised jointly to promote mutual rapprochement between historical churches and charismatic congregations.

Local events can also be used as regular ecumenical dates for various congregations. It can become a matter of course that Christians of other denominations are officially invited to special events at church and welcomed publicly. This may well lead to joint celebrations, organised each time by a different congregation in the town or district. The ecumenical intention is also served when such encounters are announced in advance and reported in the media. When fairs and festivals are organised by others, for example by the municipal authorities, local churches of different denominations can make a joint appearance.

The desire for ecumenical solidarity can be particularly signalised by the joint celebration of worship services – for example on Whit Monday. In any case, an appropriate way of getting to know each other should be offered beforehand, in order to reduce the experiences of lasting strangeness and increase the feeling of ecumenical fellowship.

Learning from social services

In the field of social service and welfare work, the boundaries and distinctions between different denominations have become even less significant. The people working in the area of German Protestant social services (*Diakonie*) now come from all denominations. Even the stipulation of membership in one of the ACK churches as a prerequisite for an employment contract is not applied everywhere. Thus, those who are serious about their Christian faith and consciously represent the Christian profile of *Diakonie* often come closer to one another. Sometimes they form a completely new ecumenical fellowship that has a positive effect on the atmosphere among the mixed staff of an institution or organisation.

The member institutions within the regional Protestant social service agencies also include those of Pentecostal-charismatic origin. When a congregation comes into contact at this level, recognising the ecumenical diversity in the diaconal landscape and linking up with it, that can also open doors to Pentecostal-charismatic Christians.

Finally, one can refer to the experience of chaplains, deacons and social workers in diaconal institutions who meet with clients, patients, migrants, people in need and many others. Here there is a wide range of conversations on every kind of topic, including faith and spirituality. One should take advantage of such colleagues as special experts on the ecumenical surroundings of a local church or a church district. They should be invited to share their knowledge and experience, for example at pastors' conferences.

Shaping social space

Diaconal projects on the local church level, such as an international café, a bicycle repair shop, a shared social lunch, etc., offer points of contact with people from a Pentecostal-charismatic tradition, often with a migration background. This can lead to cooperation with neighbouring Pentecostals and their congregations. A joint analysis of the potential in the social space could, for example, help the local Protestant and Pentecostal congregations to work together as joint actors.

Being a host

Further to that, ecumenical relations can serve to share church premises. Pentecostal or Charismatic congregations often hold their services at different times from mainstream churches, or they are willing to alter their service times if they are offered the opportunity to hold them in the local church building. This kind of hospitality is already practised in many places. It would be a wasted opportunity if contacts were limited to technical matters such as rent payments or cleaning the rooms. A church that rents rooms to another Christian group should take an interest in its guests. The hosts should know the name of the renting congregation and be able to assess its theological profile; they should know and be able to pronounce the names of the people in charge. Everyone would profit from a contact going beyond formal agreements. Guests should also take an interest in their hosts. By the way, one can also become a guest in one's own house by accepting invitations from the "tenants" and occasionally attending their services. For this task, there could be contact pilots in the congregation who first take on this important ecumenical task on behalf of others and then share their experiences in the congregation.

However, it can also be very helpful if the leaders, pastors and preachers of the different congregations meet at regular intervals for an interdenominational and international conference, an opportunity for internal theological discussion and common prayer for the people in the neighbourhood which the various churches share.

Accompanying refugees

Many Pentecostal churches in Germany are intercultural congregations. Their members often have a migration background. This fact, but also the imperative of practical solidarity, can promote the accomplishment of joint tasks in the field of humanitarian or social work in ecumenical unity, whilst also exchanging views on issues of theology and belief.

Pastoral work and support can take many different forms, depending on the circumstances and resources. Many parishes already offer round tables. They promote language skills and can also provide psychosocial support for people with a migration or refugee background. Where people share their individual stories, the conversation and companionship can also develop into a shared "spiritual journey" and a mutual learning process that empowers both sides.

Sharing social responsibility in the region

Ecumenism is always also active ecumenism. The joint assumption of responsibility for social coexistence, for justice, peace and the integrity of creation in the concrete local context as well as regionally and worldwide serves to deepen ecumenical encounter. At the same time, the common struggle against racism and violence and the commitment to human rights, cultural and religious diversity, reconciliation, peace and sustainable living conditions for the whole of creation is a visible ecumenical sign of Christian love for our neighbours, bearing witness to our common hope and obligation. This requires on both sides a patient and persistent willingness to learn.

5.3 Institutionalising ecumenical dialogues – the level of the church's governing bodies

Official talks

With the Charta Oecumenica (2001), the Christian churches in Europe commit themselves "to act together at all levels of church life wherever conditions permit and there are no reasons of faith or overriding expediency mitigating against this" (Guideline 4). A precondition for the practical realisation of this guideline is clear agreement on official discussions between the church leadership bodies of different denominations. When it comes to Pentecostal churches, charismatic congregations and international Pentecostal groups, there is also a need for an institutional dialogue framework.

Apart from multilateral cooperation at the various levels of the ACK and the dialogue between the representatives of the EKD and the Association of Protestant Free Churches in Germany (VEF) – also a kind of multilateral dialogue, since the VEF unites different traditions –, bilateral talks with the → Association of Pentecostal Churches and the → Mülheim Association should take place in regular meetings of a contact committee. It should be noted that in addition to the large number of organised Pentecostal congregations, there are a great many charismatically oriented congregations that do not belong to any umbrella organisation but nonetheless feel that they belong to a German or international network.

The discussions aim to overcome traditional theological judgments or condemnations. Pentecostal churches are described as "sects" – by people from the regional Protestant churches, or the established churches are allegedly un-Christian or even anti-Christian groups – from the Pentecostal point of view; such comments are inappropriate and violate the call of the gospel to fellowship and reconciliation.

In recent years, particular attention has been paid to the significance of baptism in the various churches, especially to the requests for baptism on the part of asylum seekers. An important document of the bilateral dialogue between the EKD and the VEF was published in 2013, the joint handout for local parishes dealing with such requests (*"Zum Umgang mit Taufbegehren von Asylsuchenden"*), in which representatives of various Pentecostal churches participated. Both sides have benefited from the theological dialogue and have committed themselves to an attitude that is neither determined by restraint that denies baptism to people who ask for it, nor by an ecumenically reckless mission strategy that gives in to a request for baptism without examining whether it is backed by serious faith.[42]

Shared responsibility for religious education

There is also a need for clarification at the institutional level. What role can and do Pentecostal churches want to play in the responsibility for religious education in schools? How can arrangements be made regarding the accreditation of teachers of religious education without insisting that the candidates convert to another denomination? It is also necessary to find a common positive attitude towards the curricula which qualify teachers of religion. It is to be considered how the Pentecostal

---

42 For the current status of the talks between the EKD and VEF on the topic of baptism, see German language epd-Dokumentation 14/2020.

movement in Germany can participate actively in the training of teachers of religion and how they can help to give the subject Religion a positive image in the schools. This is particularly important since there are now quite a few schoolchildren with a Pentecostal/Charismatic background in the classes for religious education, whose decisive attitude to the instructional material presents a major challenge for many teachers.

Research projects

The academic study of the history, faith practice and theologies of other confessions must continue to play an important role at the national EKD level. The Institute for Inter-Confessional Research in Bensheim, the Institute for Research on Religious and Ideological Issues and the Mission Academy at the University of Hamburg accentuate with their academic groundwork for ecumenical dialogue an appropriate balance between ecumenical rapprochement and theological critique. The EKD will only be able to meet the challenge and shape ecumenism as long as qualified further training is also offered at this level to create the conditions for dialogue and there is an academic contribution to a continuing and competent knowledge of the Pentecostal movement in Germany and the rest of the world. Many of the contributions in this study document are based on research provided by the institutions mentioned. Many knowledgeable ecumenists have gained their competence through contact with these important institutions.

Official seminars for church leaders can also sharpen mutual understanding and deepen the ecumenical relationship. The ACK Germany as "National Church Council" could be the appropriate forum for such study meetings. These formats for negotiation could tie in with the existing study projects of the national ACK and at the same time give the central worship services and events of the ACK a theological foundation and strengthen their official church legitimacy.

Furthermore, the development of common study documents strengthens ecumenical cooperation and can be a model for ecumenism at the local, regional and international levels. Co-operation of church leadership beyond the regional borders could be integrated into the intercultural process of the regional Protestant churches and strengthen it in turn.

5.4 Joint world responsibility – Global ecumenism and project work

Church agencies in the field of development, ecumenism and mission need criteria of coherence in theology, ecumenism, development and human rights issues as well as institutional reliability and capacity. Where cooperation results in a functional added value for the achievement of the generally agreed goals for development, ecumenism or ecumenical mission, it makes sense to be open for such cooperation with Pentecostal churches and networks. This is especially true for Pentecostal churches which are already part of regional or international structures of ecumenical cooperation and which are recommended by their ecumenical partners for further continuation. In cooperation with the Protestant development and relief agency *Brot für die Welt* (Bread for the World), the *Evangelische Mission Weltweit – EMW* (Association of Protestant Churches and Missions in Germany) and the regional mission agencies, one can identify the following important ecumenical partnerships and projects in the fields of development, ecumenism and mission.

Suggestions for cooperation with Pentecostal partner organisations in exchange with partner churches

For the project work of *Brot für die Welt* and the sister organisation *Diakonie Katastrophenhilfe*, *EMW* and the international mission fellowships and agencies in Germany associated with it, the ecumenical partner churches and organisations should seek to share and stabilise their various experiences with Pentecostal churches. Partner churches with which the EKD or its member churches are closely connected through partnership agreements and long-standing ecumenical relationships are contributors to the ecumenical dialogue about and with Pentecostal churches and the Pentecostal movement worldwide. Partner churches abroad have a special expertise with regard to charismatic and Pentecostal groups and congregations in their neighbourhood[43] and have their own perspective on the orientation of the respective Pentecostal congregations in their context. On the basis of local experience, they develop their own assessments of the openness of Pentecostal churches in their context to ecumenical dialogue with other churches or to development networks as well as to their behaviour towards people of other religions or no religion. Corresponding assessments can also be obtained from mission and partnership organisations (ecumenical organisations). When visiting

---

43 See for example the study of the ACT Ecumenical Forum in South America: *Magali Do Nascimento Cunha*, Fundamentalisms, the Crisis of Democracy and the Threat to Human Rights in South America: Trends and Challenges for Action, Salvador (Bahia) 2020, or the UEM consultation "Pentecostal Movement: A Challenge to Traditional Churches in Africa" in September 2019 in Douala, Cameroon.

partner churches, delegations can express their interest in the Pentecostal environment. They can stimulate intercultural exchange about particular challenges with regard to Pentecostalism or even participate in ecumenical developments in the neighbourhood of the partner churches. Possible conflicts in the immediate vicinity should not be underestimated. In many regions of the Global South, the neighbourhood to Pentecostal churches is extremely ambivalent, especially for historical Protestant churches. One should refrain from offering advice on ecumenical fellowship to partner churches, but the exchange of impressions, mutual perception and consultation can deepen the partnership.

⊙ Case study: Evangelical Lutheran Church of Papua New Guinea

The Evangelical Lutheran Church of Papua New Guinea (ELCPNG) has experienced various waves of religious movements since the arrival of Christianity in the 19th century. Traditional, Pentecostal and charismatic movements have emerged both within and outside the church and have had a major impact on the conventional forms of mission and worship in the Lutheran Church. Characteristic for more recent charismatic movements is their need for religious identity and their emphasis on power and prosperity. The followers of charismatic groups consider the traditional Lutheran forms of worship to be irrelevant because no recognisable power emanates from them. They feel that the mainstream church is formal, regulated and intellectual, and thus unattractive and exclusive. Instead, they are looking for a Spirit-filled church whose piety is dynamic, lively and inclusive.

Already in the 1970s, the ELCPNG experienced a first wave of Pentecostalisation with the arrival of Pentecostal missionaries from the USA. At the beginning of the 1990s, a wave of charismatisation also began within the Lutheran Church. It was initiated by a man from the Netherlands who worked as a mission teacher in the ELCPNG. The movement began at a church school for evangelists where he was teaching and soon sparked a great religious wave throughout the church. Driven by the desire for *a new life, a new church and the power of the Holy Spirit,* followers claimed that baptism in water was no more than a ritual of repentance, but that baptism in the Holy Spirit was necessary for true salvation in Christ.

Large → crusades took place in various places, attracting even more people. One of these crusades reached an estimated 10,000 people. Soon the movement spread and conquered new territories. The impact on mainstream Lutheran congregations in these areas was enormous, and their membership declined as a result. Representatives of the mainstream Lutheran group accused the charismatics of becoming too emotional and leading people astray with distorted theologies and disorderly worship services.

When the movement reached its peak, the church leaders reacted – but not all in the same way. While some of them acknowledged the movement, others felt that charismatic thinking called traditional Lutheran teachings and practices into question. They were concerned that the charismatic movement would threaten the unity of the ELCPNG. The former bishop, Sir Getake Gam, criticised and rejected the movement outright, because he considered its basic ideas to be incompatible with Lutheran doctrine. The charismatic groups endangered the cohesion of the church. Gam expelled the charismatic leaders from the church. On the other hand, another former bishop, Dr. Wesley Kigasung, considered the charismatic movement to be valuable and called for dialogue between "new Lutherans" and mainstream Lutherans. He believed that despite all differences, the designation "Lutheran" was the common denominator and should hold the two groups together. He noted that about 20 percent of Lutherans had joined the renewal groups, but still wanted to remain "Lutherans".

A dialogue office was set up: two pastors and a team took on the task of promoting dialogue between the two groups. Various consultations and conferences were organised in the hope of reuniting the two groups. Finally, a big conference called "Conference of Coming Together" was organised for discussion. Holy Communion was celebrated together. It was a hopeful sign of reconciliation. But after the conference nothing happened; and unfortunately the dialogue office was closed. The initiative came to a standstill: some of the charismatics did indeed rejoin the Lutheran mainstream, bringing with them new energy and piety. Others, however, remained undeterred and formed their own church. This church does not yet have its own name, but wants to continue to be associated with Luther, to identify with the history of the Lutheran Reformation and, in doing so, to express anew faith in the power of the Holy Spirit.

In retrospect, it is clear that people were searching for new meaning and identity within the same Lutheran family. In the meantime, the Lutheran Renewal Church exists alongside the Lutheran mainstream church. It has its own leadership, its own administrative structures and a training institution for pastors. Because they feel themselves to be an offshoot of the mainstream church, their members contin- ue to see themselves as Lutherans. The mainstream Luther- ans, however, reject their charismatic orientation. Dialogue is an ongoing challenge.

Charismatic elements are still present within the ELCPNG today. Pastors and church members adopt new charismatic forms in their congregational services. The liturgical free- dom of the charismatics seems attractive to them. They find it more appealing and lively than the rigid, fixed form. Such challenges and experiences pose an important question for the Lutheran Church today: how can the Lutheran heritage, its values and identity be preserved in a rapidly changing church and society?

In recent years, consultations to which the EKD or the regional churches and their mission agencies have jointly invited part- ner churches together with their ecumenical neighbours have proved to be particularly instructive and positive for building up relationships. For example, there was a joint study process of leaders from partner churches of the EKD and Pentecostal churches from Latin America, which took place in Wittenberg in 2011.[44] In joint consultations, it is possible to exchange views on relevant themes of theology, practical theology and church politics. In such a trilateral debate, sensitive topics can be discussed, such as the → Prosperity gospel or a "health and wealth" theology, the understanding of an appropriate rela- tionship between church and politics, and the question of the relationship between eschatology and ethics.

---

44 Wie uns der Geist bewegt. Erfahrungen in der Begegnung mit lateinamerikanischen Pfingst- kirchen (Blaue Reihe No. 16), ed. EMW, Hamburg 2013.

⊙ Case study: Evangelical Lutheran Church in Tanzania

Most of the Christian churches in Tanzania were influenced in some way by the East African revival movement – the WALOKOLE – by which charismatic groupings spread to both mainline and Pentecostal churches.

The Evangelical Lutheran Church (ELCT) is one of the largest and fastest growing Lutheran churches in Tanzania. It was formed on 19 June 1963 through the merger of the seven independent Lutheran churches that had already been cooperating in the Federation of Lutheran Churches in Tanganyika since 1955. The charismatic character of the ELCT is very pronounced and strong in its dioceses in urban areas such as Dar es Salaam, Arusha, Mbeya and Mwanza. In general, charismatisation within the ELCT is mainly an urban phenomenon. It particularly affects and shapes the Eastern and Coastal Diocese with the largest city in Tanzania, Dar es Salaam. The Eastern and Coastal Diocese consists of 93 parishes and numbers about 350,000 members with 114 pastors. Since the late 1970s, but increasingly since the mid-1990s, members of the Eastern and Coastal Diocese have joined charismatic groups. They declared that the classical Lutheran liturgy had become irrelevant to them and was particularly ineffective in cases of demon possession. From then on, some attended both Lutheran and charismatic services, while others left the ELCT altogether. To stop the loss of members, the Lutheran Church adopted some charismatic practices in its services. The pastors were urged to pay more attention to the spiritual needs of the members of their congregations, to take more time for prayer and preaching the Word of God. Some Lutheran parishes in Dar es Salaam became charismatic in this way, including the

Kimara congregation, the Kijitonyama congregation known as "Megachurch: The School of Healing", the Mbezi Beach congregation and the Mbezi Luis congregation known as "Mountain of Hope". They celebrated "deliverance services" with demon exorcisms, which do not normally exist in the Lutheran Church. They healed and did other miracles in the name of Jesus – barren women had children, unemployed people found a job.

In these "Lutheran-charismatic" congregations – especially those located on main roads and in the city centre – services were now held in the early morning and in the evening under the title "Morning Glory" and "Evening Glory". This mission strategy was very convenient for commuters in the big city: Lutheran parishioners could easily attend the short prayer times on their way to work or back home.

The main doctrine was the → Prosperity gospel or the "word of faith", a proclamation revolving around prosperity, success, spiritual warfare and healing, which is always God's wish for his people. Faith, talking positively, and donations to religious causes would increase material prosperity. It was emphasised that Christ's death freed people not only from sin, but also from sickness and poverty.

These churches expanded quickly – spiritually, numerically and financially. Some streamed their services online (e.g. *Eliona Kimaro TV*, also on YouTube), others built schools or hospitals, some even offered scholarships for students at home and abroad. The participation is ecumenical: not only Lutherans attend the services, but also Pentecostals, Anglicans, Baptists, Moravians and Catholics. Sometimes even Muslims come (there is a 40-day period of prayer and fasting in the Kimara congregation).

Charismatisation in the Eastern and Coastal Diocese is a complex and multidimensional process. It affects the ELCT and the lives of its members not only theologically and spiritually, but also socially and economically. Today, the ELCT has "Charismatic Lutheran congregations", "Lutheran megachurches" and Lutheran "Deliverance centres". One of the latter is the Lutheran congregation of Kimara, whose services are attended by more than 5,000 people every week, with average Sunday collections of more than 10,000 euros. Their services are very lively, with many young people, both men and women, taking part. Lay people are involved in the service; they do the preaching, the praise and the prayers of deliverance. Nevertheless, the charismatisation in the Eastern and Coastal Diocese is also apparently a unique trend within the ELCT, which is sometimes viewed very critically by many Christians in other dioceses due to negative ecumenical experiences with neighbouring Pentecostal churches.

By talking to ecumenical partner churches and listening to the experiences in their country, it is possible to develop helpful criteria for dealing with Pentecostal churches in specific regions. In addition, this can be the start of processes of transformation in the regional ecumenical debate, for example with regard to fundamentalism and misleading theologies.

Active role of the EKD in the WCC and the Global Christian Forum (GCF)

The basic statement of the WCC in 1991 applies to all member churches of the WCC. The EKD is therefore involved in the implementation of the decisions. This includes the following points:

Dialogue with Pentecostal churches takes place on various levels. First of all, it is necessary to distinguish between these levels. There are some Pentecostal churches that are open to the ecumenical movement and others that are critical of the ecumenical movement. The WCC is committed to remaining in dialogue with both groups in different ways. In general, Pentecostal churches are invited to participate in WCC programmes – especially in the Faith and Order Commission and the Commission on Word Mission and Evangelism. Everyone should make sure that members of Pentecostal churches are included when planning the services at the Assemblies.

With regard to the → Global Christian Forum, there are the following commitments: to evaluate the work done so far in the Joint Consultative Group of the WCC and Pentecostals, which has been in existence since 2000, and to deepen its work. The focus is on controversial issues in the area of social ethics, political ethics, practical witness for peace, justice and integrity of creation, and the role of different forms of the → Prosperity gospel. Going beyond that, issues of peace, justice and climate justice of all the world's Christian churches must be on the agenda of the GCF at a time of planetary ecological crisis. Finally, there is a need to work together on a differentiated statement on the political instrumentalisation of religion through fundamentalism and populism. The WCC Assembly in Karlsruhe in 2022 can formulate guiding recommendations, also on the initiative of the German delegation.

Here one must point out the demand for assistance and better cooperation with Pentecostal churches with regard to qualified theological training which is capable of dialogue. This is to be mentioned separately below.

5.5 Strengthening academic hospitality – Ecumenism with Pentecostals in theology and theological education

Support for international students and tapping into their competences

At the Mission Academy of the University of Hamburg, at the University of Applied Sciences for Intercultural Theology (FIT, in cooperation with the University of Göttingen) and at other locations, students from Pentecostal churches in the Global South are supported in graduate and postgraduate programmes. They are part of ecumenical learning communities in which they themselves bring in their (faith) experiences and their theological reflections. Scholarship programmes, which do not strictly adhere to the stipulation that only members of WCC member churches may be sponsored, make an enormous contribution to the theological understanding between Pentecostalism and ecumenical Christianity. The Pentecostal students at the University of Applied Sciences for Intercultural Theology and the Mission Academy provide important inspiration and expertise for ecumenical understanding in Germany. They introduce new topics and perspectives from their home countries into theology; they demonstrate the differences between the religious landscape in Germany and the conditions where completely different majorities and minorities exist. The scholarship programme, which is financed by *Brot für die Welt* and the EMW among others, is to be expanded, especially in the area of support for Pentecostal theologians and professors.

At the ⊙ Theological Seminary in Erzhausen, about 40 percent of Pentecostal students come from countries of the Global

South, most of whom have a background of migration. Unfortunately, up to now neither side has made any significant efforts to organise an exchange between the university faculties and the Pentecostal Theological Seminary in Germany and enable the students to make ecumenical encounters.

Pentecostal theology students – whether in the context of the classical theological training courses or at the Pentecostal seminary – should be regularly given a chance to speak as experts and be integrated normally into further education and seminar activities at academies and institutes in all parts of the EKD. They represent a unique network of speakers.

Cooperation in teaching and research

Members of Pentecostal churches are already studying at the faculties of Protestant Theology at state universities and at church universities of applied sciences with the aim of going into church leadership or school education. At the same time, quite a few Protestant theology students from EKD member churches who are training for pastoral service or teaching in schools are interested in charismatic and Pentecostal piety and looking for personal experiences in this area. On the practical level, one can see that ecumenism has already overtaken the institutionalised forms of theological education. It is therefore all the more urgent for those responsible for theological education to think about the chances and limits of cooperation. They should consider jointly the possibilities of devising practically orientated theological study courses in ecumenical cooperation with Pentecostal churches. The deliberate integration of Pentecostal theologians in individual courses or in the teaching programme should no longer be the exception. Ecumenical and intercultural competence and language skills are core qualifications for students, both in the academic and in the practical training phases. In a plural and globalised world, ever higher demands are being placed on future multipliers of religious themes and attitudes, particularly in this respect.[45]

These impulses follow the logic of ecumenical hospitality on an academic level. Ecumenism is practised and exemplified. Pentecostal lecturers are invited as guest lecturers or researchers. In particular, the exchange with the Pentecostal training centre in Erzhausen is to be examined and deepened. Further formats for ecumenical cooperation in the theological training of future pastors and in teacher training are thematic study projects, for which existing academic research networks such as → GloPent can be used. In addition, study trips abroad are suitable for gaining first-hand experience of a different religious landscape and studying it. These should receive greater and, above all, less bureaucratic financial support.

---

45 There is reference to these increasing demands in the recommendations of the EKD Advisory Commission for Worldwide Ecumenism in its paper "Ökumene in der evangelisch-theologischen Aus- und Fortbildung in Deutschland" (Ecumenism in Protestant theological education and training in Germany), published by the Evangelische Kirche in Deutschland (EKD), Hanover 2021. Cf. the preparatory conference volume „Die Zukunft der theologischen Ausbildung ist ökumenisch. Interkulturelle und interkonfessionelle Herausforderungen in Universität and Schule, Kirche und Diakonie", ed. by *Ulrike Link-Wieczorek, Wilhelm Richebächer* and *Olaf Waßmuth* (BÖR 127), Leipzig 2020.

6. Summary

Taking the work of the Holy Spirit as a starting point means that God's work in Jesus Christ is considered to be relevant in the practice of our present-day life. God's history with humanity reaches down into our present and future, from the creation of the world to the redemption in Jesus Christ and the hope of the Kingdom of God. Otherwise Christian faith would make no sense. A closer look at the Pentecostal movement and at charismatic believers challenges the historical confessional churches to reconsider this credo. Just like many Pentecostals, we have questions to ask. Does our life change when we put our faith in God's present work? How do we perceive the world from this perspective? But apart from such questions we may have new doubts. If God is active in the present, what does that mean for our intercessions? Do Pentecostal and charismatic believers have helpful answers?

This study document helps to provide orientation about the church family which exists in Germany as a "Pentecostal movement" and as Pentecostal churches with a migrant background, although not all of these churches feel that they belong to "one family". The Pentecostal movement manifests itself in a special way as a global phenomenon and appears in an impressive variety of forms and theological interpretations of the Holy Spirit. It provokes a post-Enlightenment theological self-confidence through forms of ecstatic spiritual experience and unswerving trust in God. Its diversity ranges from the basic trait of pious devotion to God to the downright command to God in summoning his action. The diversity of Pentecostal churches in Germany and the world is demonstrated in some contexts by the heightened self-confidence of previously marginalised sections of the population, in other contexts by the emergence of economically strong megachurches claiming great power through the media. Here, the invocation of the Holy Spirit nurtures political calculation which is conscious of its power. It is precisely this diversity that can lead to uncertainty and a general attitude of rejection on the part of a traditional church culture. There is a probable connection with a tradition of undifferentiated condemnation of Anabaptist churches going back to the Reformation, which experienced a reassessment in 2010 in the Lutheran-Mennonite dialogue document "Healing Memories: Reconciling in Christ".

This study document wants to pay differentiated and critical attention and help strengthen Reformation identity in its diversity. It seeks to avoid an attitude of blanket refusal of dialogue and relies on the conviction that credible and enriching learning partnerships can arise when historical Protestant churches and Pentecostal churches and other charismatic forms of piety meet up with one another. These opportunities for encounter do not happen by chance, but must be actively sought by both sides. In this sense, the study document is directed at those who bear responsibility in the churches and organisations of the EKD, urging them to carefully examine and diligently shape this opportunity for dialogue in their own regions and also on the worldwide level, with the help of their partner churches and institutions. This document is intended to encourage people to consider the theological opportunities and challenges of dialogue with Pentecostal believers from the local church level upwards. In the face of an increasing cultural forgetfulness of God, it seeks to encourage the churches to develop jointly with

Pentecostals a new quality of communication with reference to one's own faith. The study document also wants to encourage willing Pentecostal churches to become possible dialogue partners for important topics in the social-ethical agencies of the EKD working for a safe, sustainable and just life for all people. For this purpose, preliminary test criteria are proposed to which the partners can mutually appeal. These should exclude a possible instrumentalisation of the gospel for goals contrary to human rights or the justification of autocratic regimes and leadership styles, whilst at the same time preventing existing ecumenical partner relationships of Protestant churches in certain regions from being harmed by uncoordinated relationships with new partners. The document also suggests that in the future work of its international dialogue commission with Pentecostal churches, the WCC should pay greater attention to the open questions of possibilities and limits of common socio-ethical orientation and work.

The study document is thus theologically open and interested in dialogue when it looks for potential common basic elements of Christian faith tradition that are shared with the Pentecostal movement. It tries to understand what is strange and different, and at the same time seeks critical demarcation where the truth of the Protestant faith and the integrity of the Christian witness for justice, peace and the integrity of creation are at stake, or where the commitment to human dignity is endangered.

The best way forward with this text is that Christians from different backgrounds and perspectives, from regional mainstream churches, free churches, charismatic and Pentecostal congregations can come to speak with each other on some of the topics of this study and thus enter into a relationship with each other. It would be good if this study document could motivate people to discover added value and promise in such meetings – even if it leads to critical controversy. It would be a great step for ecumenism if they were to experience in practice that honest dialogue between brothers and sisters can lead to a deepening or even to a correction of their own spiritual life and thus serve to make the common witness in the present society more credible.

Glossary

African Instituted Churches

African Instituted Churches (AICs) have been founded by indigenous African mission initiatives that broke away from the colonial mission churches and represent a new connection between African culture and Christian tradition. They are characterised by a great diversity and heterogeneous structure. Basically, two groups of AICs can be distinguished: the early, pre-colonial AICs and those that emerged in the first half of the 20th century with an anti-colonial orientation. Among the early AICs are the *Ethiopian Orthodox Church* and the *Coptic Orthodox Church* in Egypt, which can trace their origins back to the African apostle John Mark in the first century AD. It was the Coptic Pope Shenouda of Alexandria who took the initiative in founding the Organization of African Instituted Churches (OAIC) in 1978.

The majority of today's approximately 10,000 AIC denominations has emerged since the second half of the 19th century. Typical is their interest in the indigenisation of the Gospel in a post-colonial orientation. The AICs are not a uniform denominational family. Their wide range of forms is reflected in the different names that they give themselves: *Spiritual* or *Pentecostal Churches* (emphasis on the gifts of the Holy Spirit), *Apostolic Churches* (emphasis on the apostleship), *Messianic Churches* (emphasis on a quasi-messianic founder figure), *Ethiopian Movement Churches* (emphasis on African autonomy), *Zion Churches* (emphasis on indigenous African cosmology and holistic healing). In contrast to the negative assessment of African culture in the colonial era, AICs emphasise the combination of Christian charismatic elements with motifs of indigenous religiosity, dynastic leadership traditions and culture. To this day, AICs suffer from deprecation and discrimination by representatives of historical mission churches. AICs are to be found in a total of 43 countries on the African continent. In many countries of Southern Africa between 50% and 75% of the population are members of an AIC.

Azusa Street Revival

The "Azusa Street Revival" is still considered to be the "cradle" (Hollenweger) of a new, 20th century religious Christian movement with roots in the revival and Holiness movements of the 19th century (Allan H. Anderson). This definition is *historical* by the place (Azusa Street, Los Angeles) and time (14 April 1906 to May 1913), *theological* (doctrine of the baptism in the Spirit, eschatological millenarian expectation, practice of spiritual gifts), *sociological* (Apostolic Faith Mission) and *personalised* (the Afro-American preacher William J. Seymour is considered the founder).

The movement, characterised by ecstatic spiritual experiences such as miracles and speaking in tongues, was transcultural, trans-denominational, trans-social and adhered to no gender-specific stereotypes: predominantly black people together with Hispanic, white, poor and wealthy people, both men and women, "reinvented" what is handed down biblically as the "miracle of Pentecost" (Acts 2:1–13). Azusa Street, the so-called *American Jerusalem*, was something like the culmination, not the creative origin of a global expectation which had started with the Holiness movement.

Politically and sociologically, it was an oppositional movement: the participants were criticised for behaviour that was consid ered unheard of at the beginning of the 20th century. In Germany, the Protestant majority disqualified the young Pentecostal movement as heretical and spiritistic ("spirits from below") in the → Berlin Declaration of 1909.

The "Azusa Street Revival" is the discursive core or yardstick of the Pentecostal movement or the "Apostolic Faith Mission on Azusa Street", since it formed regional as well as national networks using all media of the time: centrifugally by sending missionaries, centripetally as a magnet that attracted Christian leaders. It is important that a network of faith missions, sanctification and healing movements already existed. Only this can explain the rapid spread of the Pentecostal movement.

Beyond the North American and European perspective, there were and are many "New Jerusalems" that confirmed the renewed worldwide "outpouring of the Holy Spirit" and made reciprocal references to the "Azusa Street" where it supposedly started: Pyongyang (Korea); Beijing (China); Pune (India); Wakkerstroom (South Africa); Lagos (Nigeria); Valparaiso (Chile); Oslo (Norway); Sunderland (England); Kassel (Germany).

Berlin and Kassel Declaration

At the beginning of the 20th century, when the first Pentecostal spiritual experiences in Germany became known, it caused scepticism among other churches, as in all parts of the world. In Germany, however, a particular confrontation took place, not between the main representatives of the regional Protestant churches and those of the new revival, but within the pietistic Fellowship movement of the regional churches. That is to say, the dispute was between those who placed great hopes in special spiritual experiences on the one hand, and those who issued a warning against the demonic nature of ecstatic states on the other. In 1907, a Holiness meeting took place in Kassel with guests from Norway, during which spectacular ecstatic experiences occurred. This led to an intensification of the dispute, culminating in the official condemnation of these phenomena in the so-called Berlin Declaration of 15 September 1909. The crucial sentence reads: "The so-called Pentecostal movement is not from above, but from below." In this way, the Pentecostal movement in Germany was condemned by a part of the revivalist, pietist wing in the regional churches as a work of the devil and the split within the neo-pietist Holiness movement in Germany was sealed for decades.

It was not until 1996 that the Kassel Declaration was signed, in which the representatives of the German Evangelical Alliance (Rolf Hille, Peter Strauch, Hartmut Steeb and Christoph Morgner) and the representatives of the Association of Pentecostal Churches (Ingolf Ellßel, Gottlob Ling, Gerhard Oertel and Richard Krüger) affirmed their common dogmatic basis and agreed on future cooperation. The declaration names controversial phenomena which play a role in Pentecostal piety, such as "'resting in the spirit', expelling so-called 'territorial spirits'" and others which are to be avoided at joint events.

In addition to criticising the forms of expression of the new Pentecostal piety and its notions concerning the work of the Spirit, the Berlin Declaration referred above all to the new movement's understanding of sanctification and justification. "It cannot be stressed strongly enough that one must keep an eye on sin, an eye that Is not clouded by a man-made sanctification or by an imaginary doctrine of the removal of sinful nature." Here and in other formulations, the Berlin Declaration clearly states its position and, aside from the intended dissociation from the Pentecostal movement, also delivers a strong testimony to the doctrine of justification which is the foundation of evangelical theology It is clear, however, that the greatest public effect of the document came from the fact that a part of the pietistic revival wing in the regional churches qualified the Pentecostal movement as a the work of Satan.

Crusades

The Anglophone use of the term "crusade" for urban, interdenominational mass evangelism, which has been widespread primarily in evangelical and Pentecostal Christianity since the 1950s, refers back to the images of the historic "crusades", but also reinterprets them fundamentally. Probably the first person to use the term explicitly and find countless imitators was the US Baptist preacher and evangelist *Billy Graham* (1918–2018). Far beyond the USA, he is considered one of the most influential Christian preachers of the 20th century. He himself explains the concept of the "crusades" and points out its limitations: "Mass crusades, in which I believe and to which I have committed my life, will never finish the Great Commission; but a one-by-one ministry will." Tim Beougher writes about Graham:

"Evangelistic crusades were not invented by Billy Graham, but he certainly perfected them, preaching more than 400 of them worldwide. He preached the gospel in 185 countries, to 215 million people in person, and millions more via media."

With Graham, the English crusade spread worldwide as part of the rapid expansion of the globalising Pentecostal-charismatic movement.

Crusades are a performative missionary method aimed at conversion to Christianity. The modern individual concept of conversion in evangelical Christianity can be traced back to the *Second Awakening* (a great revival movement in the USA 1800–1840). During emotional *mass rallies,* people who physically perceived the influence of the Holy Spirit began to shout, dance or cry. The acceptance of Jesus Christ as personal Saviour was seen as the beginning of a process of sanctification that involved all aspects of the believers' lives as born-again children. Emotional phenomena such as barking and dancing in the spirit, as well as the phenomenon of falling (being knocked down by the spirit), only began later. The focus was on the recognition of sin and conversion.

The public Camp Revivals and mass rallies of the *Second Awakening* in the 1820s were followed by the less emotional *Third Awakening* (1880–1910) in the 1880s. The conversions that took place here corresponded to the evangelical conversion model of repentance which had become widespread by then, embracing the acceptance of Jesus Christ as personal saviour and complete immersion in baptism. This model was consolidated by the *Holiness movement* which dominated the *Third Awakening.* The *Fourth Awakening* (1960–1980) reactivated the practices of this conversion model – for example in Billy Graham's *Crusades*.

Demons – Deliverance – Exorcism

In the global Pentecostal movement, the existence of demons is fundamentally assumed. The intensity with which one reckons with the activity of demons varies greatly depending on the cultural location and the theological character of the movement.

Demons are widely considered to be ungodly spiritual powers that threaten the lives of believers in all kinds of ways: their physical and mental health, their personal relationships, their faith in God, their plans, their professional success, etc. This belief in the existence and effect of evil spiritual forces in real life is an expression of a dualistic world view, which can rightly be based on New Testament accounts of Jesus casting out demons.

For West Africa, there is a clearly prevalent tendency within Pentecostal Christianity to demonise ambivalent spiritual beings from traditional religions, in particular those of the ancestors. This is the continuation of the widespread disqualification of African cultures by Western missionaries in the 19th and early 20th century. In the course of a current reconsideration of traditional values and cultures in West Africa, some Pentecostal churches are starting to make a critical reappraisal of this legacy. This shows that it may come to developments and changes in the views on demons in Pentecostalism.

Pentecostals can relate to Jesus' authority to cast out demons (exorcism, e.g. Mk 9:29) and the call to his disciples to do the same. They know that they are spiritually empowered to do so. When the casting out of demons by Pentecostals is described, it sometimes sounds like a re-enactment of Jesus' actions in the modern age. Pentecostals widely refer to these acts as *deliverance,* meaning liberation from disruptive spiritual forces in order to enable life in abundance. Due to global migration movements, acts of deliverance now also take place in numerous international congregations in Germany.

Fundamentalism

The term fundamentalism is applied in various fields of knowledge. It is also commonly used in civil society, politics and the media. Here it is used as a critical attribute and refers to orientations or modes of behaviour whose advocates maintain that a fundamental conviction (e. g. a canonical religious text) is binding regardless of the context and use it as the basis for their own situation and decisions. The pejorative tone which is connected with this concept of fundamentalism makes it difficult to deal with the problems it describes.

Historically, the term fundamentalism was not originally used in a pejorative sense; Christians used the term to describe themselves in the context of a series of texts entitled "The Fundamentals – A Testimony to the Truth", published in Chicago between 1909 and 1915. Its authors, who were rooted in the Young Men's Christian Association (YMCA), defended their faith and especially their understanding of the Bible against modernising influences, which they claimed were driving them out of the YMCA. The dispute concerned the historical credibility of the Bible, especially in the stories of creation and the virgin birth of

Jesus, the necessity of Jesus' substitutionary atonement on the cross, and his bodily resurrection and return. This was largely identical with the contents of the so-called Statement of Faith of the World Evangelical Alliance of 1846.

To this day, fundamentalism is widely regarded as a predominantly religious problem, insofar as political fundamentalisms can be attributed to religious motives. On the other hand, the term fundamentalism is neutral when used by academic sociology, political and religious science. In these cases, fundamentalism designates processes that counteract the typical differentiation of social functional systems in modern societies (e.g. the legal and economic systems) by founding their description on orientational differences of ideology or even personal constellations.

Critical scrutiny of pejorative terms of fundamentalism has enabled theology to come to the realisation that fundamentalism, the self-styled alternative to modernity, is on the contrary itself a project of modernity (James Barr). With its emphasis on the historical credibility of the Bible, fundamentalism pursues the same epistemological ideal as the historical criticism exercised by 19th century modernism in the European and Anglo-Saxon world with regard to the historicity of the Bible and the understanding of redemption derived from it. Both fundamentalism and modernism are close to positivist epistemology, which is based on the assumption of a correspondence between the content and object of knowledge that is independent of context and can be verified by means of objective measurement.

When describing Pentecostal Christianity, the category of fundamentalism should be used with caution, since the associated biblical practices of decontextualisation can nevertheless go hand in hand with a strongly contextual understanding of faith.

Global Christian Forum

The Global Christian Forum (GCF) is a forum for consultations that was founded in 1998 on the initiative of the World Council of Churches as an extended frame of reference. A policy paper was presented at the 8th Assembly of the WCC in Harare in 1998 proposing the establishment of an extended "forum", a suggestion that had emerged as the result of the process of reflection on the common understanding and vision of the World Council of Churches. The intention was to create a broader model of relations than existed in the community of WCC member churches and to bring these churches into a lasting ecumenical conversation with churches that are not (yet) members of the WCC. In 2002, the first consultation of the GCF was held at Fuller Theological Seminary in Pasadena, where more than 50 percent of the participating churches were non-member churches of the WCC and one of the most important expectations was that the old dividing lines between "ecumenical" and "evangelical" should be overcome. The GCF is therefore not a "counter-organisation" to the WCC, nor does it seek to be an institutional alternative or to establish a new formal ecclesial membership, but it follows a complementary approach in a broader frame of reference: Unlike the WCC, the GCF, with a small budget within the WCC budget, does not have its own programme of actions, but holds global consultations which essentially pursue the goal of contributing to the deepening of common faith convictions and the overcoming of prejudices as participants talk about the history of their faith or of their communities. Up to now, three large Global Gatherings have taken place: in 2007 in Limuru, Kenya, 2011 in Manado, Indonesia, and 2018 in Bogotá, Colombia.

GloPent: European Research Network on Global Pentecostalism

The European Research Network on Global Pentecostalism, known by the acronym GloPent, is probably the most important academic network for research into the global Pentecostal movement. GloPent is coordinated by a Steering Group consisting of researchers from six European universities (VU Amsterdam, Basel, Birmingham, Cambridge, Heidelberg, Uppsala). Founded in 2004 by Allan Anderson (Birmingham), André Droogers and Cees van der Laan (both VU Amsterdam) as well as Michael Bergunder (Heidelberg), it now comprises well over 300 registered researchers worldwide. GloPent consolidates its research network by regularly organising conferences on current research topics that are highly regarded both internationally and interdisciplinarily. Although it is primarily a European research network, the focus of its research is on contexts in the Global South. Discussion on theory and methodology of research into Pentecostalism are also promoted and published in the GloPent journal PentecoStudies. The GloPent website offers a valuable platform presenting current publications or conference papers. It also offers a resource for young researchers. Free membership in the GloPent network is open to all who are researching the global Pentecostal movement at least at the doctoral level.

Glossolalia

Glossolalia is a phenomenon described in the New Testament in connection with an extraordinary work of the Holy Spirit. Colloquially, it is translated as speaking in tongues (Greek: *glossa* = tongue/language; *lalein* = to speak) and refers to utterances that are incomprehensible and comparable to speaking in a foreign language. Pentecostal and charismatic circles are convinced that speaking in tongues not only occurred in the early Christian church, but can also play a role today in strengthening believers and developing the church.

In the Acts of the Apostles, the glossolalia is described as a recognisable sign of the presence and work of the Holy Spirit. This begins with the outpouring of the Spirit at Pentecost (Acts 2:4) and is mentioned again in passages relevant to missionary work (Acts 10:45–46; 19:6). In 1 Corinthians Paul describes speaking in tongues as a gift of God for spiritual edification and as an element of the prophetic gift. Speaking in tongues is associated with a personal language of prayer (1 Cor 14:2,4,14–15; Eph 6:18). It is used for edification (1 Cor 14:4), sometimes when the person cannot find words to bring joy or concern before God (Rom 8:26). Prophetic speech that is recognised as genuine is understood as God's message to the church. Speech in tongues is also mentioned in this context and needs to be interpreted in understandable language (1 Cor 14:3–5,13). It is important that the practice of glossolalia remains under human control (1 Cor 14:28,32,40) and that prophetic speech is always to be tested (14:29). As an inaccessible gift of God, it should not tempt people to think better of themselves (13,1 f.). Speaking in tongues is also mentioned in the Great Commission at the end of Mark's Gospel (Mk 16:17).

In Pentecostal circles, the first experience of speaking in tongues is often associated with a baptism in the Spirit; a sign of fullness in the Spirit. However, this is not a sacrament as in the case of actual baptism, but is to be understood metaphorically, as a sign of God's loving grace and empowerment for service. Charismatically oriented Christians in the historical churches often see the gift of tongues as a confirmation of the baptismal grace for deepening the faith and as an encouragement to witness openly to the gospel.

Megachurch

In the worldwide spectrum of the Charismatic-Pentecostal movement, but also in other churches, the phenomenon of so-called megachurches has been attracting great attention for quite some time. A megachurch is a large congregation with at least 2,000 regular worshippers. In terms of church sociology, the megachurch concept is based on the (often theatrical) exceptional status of the leader (usually male) and founding figure. He is regarded as the so-called leading or senior pastor, who is attributed with a charismatic appeal. He is supported by a team of full-time pastoral leaders and a large number of volunteers. Due to the particular social organisational form of charismatic authority, which all culminates in the key position of the founder-leader, the transition to a successor in such megachurches often triggers a crisis, which can lead them to dwindle or even disappear. It is noticeable that megachurches are predominantly under the leadership of one man, are well versed in the use of media and almost exclusively located in urban areas. They attract an interdenominational following, mostly comprised of younger people rooted in urban milieus. Many megachurches, especially in the Global South, have emerged in university neighbourhoods characterised by high upward social mobility.

Historically, megachurches started to emerge in 1958 with the founding of the ☉ Yoido Full Gospel Church in Seoul, South Korea, by David Yonggi Cho. Today, the church is considered the largest single congregation in the world. Since the 1970s, the scene has been dominated by North American megachurches such as Joel Osteen's Lakewood Church in Texas. It is considered the largest single church in the USA and, with its media empire, is one representative of the gamut of so-called television churches (→ Televangelism). Thanks to structures of international networking, the megachurch concept started to gain a foothold in the Global South in the 1980s. Here the focus of megachurch presence is currently in East and West Africa, China and South Korea. The largest single church in Europe is the Embassy of the Blessed Kingdom of God for All Nations, founded in 1993 in Kiev (Ukraine) by the Nigerian Sunday Adelaja. The church primarily shone through its programmes of social care. Adelaja is a representative of the → Prosperity gospel and has become highly controversial due to political, financial and moral incidents. The ☉ Hillsong Church, founded in Sydney in 1983, is well known in Germany. It became internationally popular through its distinctive music culture. The Lighthouse Chapel International, founded in Accra (Ghana) in 1989 by Dag Heward-Mills (whose mother comes from Basel), has several branches in Germany and is setting up a continental hub in Switzerland with its congregations there.

Mülheim Association of Free Evangelical Churches

The Mülheim Association emerged out of the pietistic Gnadau Fellowship movement within the Protestant church and belongs historically to a range of Christian groups that experienced a renewal of their faith and their fellowship in the first decade of the 20th century due to extraordinary spiritual gifts. The manifestations of the Spirit took place in groups that gathered in Mülheim/Ruhr across the boundaries of the regional Protestant church, Christian fellowships and free churches; they eventually separated from the Gnadau Association (→ Berlin Declaration of 1909). The initiators of the movement were the Protestant pastors Ernst Modersohn, Martin Girkon, Jonathan Paul and Emil Humburg as well as the revivalist preacher Jakob Vetter.

Although the Mülheim Association was originally the oldest German association of Pentecostal congregations, it is now part of the evangelical-charismatic spectrum and is no longer a member of the Forum of Free Church Pentecostal Churches since 2002. The Association is in Germany a member of the Council of Churches (ACK) and the Association of Protestant Free Churches (VEF). It also belongs to the German Evangelical Alliance, the Association of Evangelical Missions and the Circle of Charismatic Leaders. The latter brings together representatives of the Roman Catholic Church, the Protestant church, the Methodists, Baptists, free congregations, other free churches and various organisations, who meet regularly to discuss current issues in the charismatic movement in Germany. In 2009, a joint declaration was adopted by the Gnadau and Mülheim Associations in which the condemnations of the → Berlin Declaration of 1909 are no longer considered relevant for current relations and cooperation within the Evangelical Alliance.

Mukti Revival

The term Mukti Revival usually refers to two revivals that are said to have taken place between 1905 and 1907 in the Mukti Mission near Pune, founded by the Indian activist for women's rights, Pandita Ramabai (1858–1922). The Mukti Revival is regarded by some historians as the beginning of the Pentecostal movement in India – a thesis which, however, cannot be clearly proven historically, as the following explanations show.

Ramabai, who came from a Brahmin family, had already caused a stir at a young age for protesting against the patriarchal structures where she was brought up. During her medical studies in England (from 1883), she was baptised as an Anglican, but soon came into conflict with the church authorities. As a representative of the Indian women's movement, she then travelled through the United States, where she came into contact with emancipatory circles of the revivalist movement there. She returned to India in 1889. Here she established a school for the shelter and education of outcast widows and orphans.

In 1904, Ramabai and her closest colleague, the US Methodist Minnie Abrams (1859–1912), learned about the Welsh Revival, which was part of the British Holiness movement. Under this impression, a similar revival occurred a year later among some of the residents of the Mukti Mission. After the two mission leaders heard about the → Azusa Street Revival in Los Angeles at the end of 1906, another revival finally took place in the mission station in the summer of the following year, during which the phenomenon of speaking in tongues (→ glossolalia) is said to have occurred. While Abrams welcomed this innovation and joined the Pentecostal movement after her return to the USA in

1908, Ramabai was much more reserved about tongues and emphasised the emancipatory potential of the revival for the Indian church. Consequently, at the end of her life, she handed the Mukti Mission over to the Christian and Missionary Alliance (CMA) – an organisation of the "classical" Holiness movement.

Pentecostal World Fellowship

In 1947, a worldwide gathering of Pentecostal preachers and church leaders was convened for the first time, with 3,000 people moved by the Spirit coming together in Zurich. Since then, these gatherings have taken place at three-year intervals in many places around the globe. In 1961, the Pentecostal World Fellowship (PWF) was founded at the 6th conference in Jerusalem. Some of the very first protagonists were Leonhard Steiner (Swiss Pentecostal Mission), J. Roswell Flower (co-founder of the ⊙ Assemblies of God), David J. du Plessis (originally from the South African Apostolic Faith Mission, then lecturer in the USA, outstanding ecumenist of the Pentecostal movement) and Donald Gee (born in England, later lecturer in Australia, also ecumenically committed). In 1947, "The Pentecost" was founded as the published organ of the worldwide Pentecostal movement.

From 2010 to 2019, the PWF was under the presidency of Dr. Prince Guneratnam. He leads the Calvary Church in Kuala Lumpur/Malaysia. His congregation founded the Calvary Convention Centre, which serves various purposes as a trade fair building, but is used above all, with its 5,000-seat auditorium, for worship assemblies. Prince Guneratnam was also decisively involved in the → Global Christian Forum, an ecumenical network of WCC churches and the charismatic movement. Their

25th conference was held in Calgary, Canada, in 2019 under the theme "Spirit Now". The conference focused on evangelism and mission, charitable and humanitarian work, and Christian unity. In addition, a "Christian Unity Commission" was founded with the intention of promoting ecumenical dialogue between Pentecostal churches and other Christian churches and fellowships.

The PWF's nine principles of faith establish a strong reference to biblical truth (1), belief in the triune God (2), the deity of Jesus (3–4), the workings of the Holy Spirit (5–6), the universal resurrection (7), the unity of all believers (8), and the duty of Christians to care not only for the spiritual well-being of their neighbour, but also for their social, political and physical well-being (9).

Prophecy

Pentecostals believe that people can receive special insights from God through the Holy Spirit, which they are to pass on to other people. This refers, among other passages, to 1 Corinthians 14, where prophecy is listed among the gifts of the Spirit and is even rated higher than speaking in tongues. In Pentecostal practice, prophecy occurs in various ways: as a vocal utterance by individuals at a time of prayer, as a "translation" of tongues, as a proclamation from the pulpit, or as a diagnostic "utterance of knowledge" in the prayer for healing. In terms of content, Pentecostal prophecies range from general words of encouragement and vague indications of God's action to specific statements about the future, the end times or the presence of certain diseases. Personal prophecies are also given, both in private prayer times and in special services where recognised prophets share personal "words from God" with individuals.

Pentecostal prophecy is not, however, devoid of criticism. Dazzling prophets who attract attention in large gatherings and mass media are often subject to strong criticism, especially since they are already institutionally in competition with the "mainstream" of the Pentecostal movement. In general, Pentecostals believe that human craving for recognition or even demonic influences can cause false prophetic speech. Therefore, reference is often made to the need for discernment of spirits, which can provide a kind of critical counter-analysis. This is based, among other things, on the truthfulness of the prophetic statement (as far as can be judged) and on its "fruits", i. e. the nature of its effects on the life of the church and its members. Because of the danger of abuse, prophetic speech is regulated to varying degrees in different Pentecostal churches. Common to all Pentecostals, however, is the recognition of the possibility of prophetic speech, since this corresponds to the fundamental Pentecostal conviction that God's Spirit speaks to the individual and the congregation in their respective concrete situations and equips them for service in God's kingdom.

Prosperity gospel, Prosperity theology

The so-called prosperity gospel designates a tradition of interpretation according to which the attainment of worldly success, individual well-being and material prosperity is considered proof of God's blessing. Sometimes, therefore, historical theological analogies are drawn with Calvinism. However, for Pentecostal piety inspired by prosperity theology, triumphant acts of faith and confession are characteristic, and they are especially open to miraculous experience, attest to promises fulfilled and express in ritual form expectations of a better life in the material sense through divine intervention, which are considered legitimate. This hermeneutic diametrically reverses the option for the poor of liberation theology and spiritualises wealth. The roots of the Pentecostal prosperity gospel go back to the North American "Health and Wealth" circles of the period after World War II, since when it has spread world wide, especially through Pentecostal networks. Since the late 1970s, it has probably been the most ardently contested theological controversy in contemporary Christianity. It is mainly criticised by New Testament exegesis, but to a large extent also contradicts the prophetic corpus of Scripture or ascetic traditions in church history. Nevertheless, the prosperity gospel has emerged as a virtually canonised corpus of theology, especially in the Global South. Different variants can be identified. For example, under precarious social conditions it appears in the guise of an everyday "theology of survival" (or "slum" theology). Or prosperity theology addresses the increasingly emerging social middle classes in the sense of a "management Christianity" that provides instructions for successful economic action. In this respect, prosperity theology can have a socially transformative effect, whereby its authoritative advice often seems to support neo-liberal ideals of society. Its appeal here goes far beyond the Pentecostal movement and finds a lively echo in the various denominational families; in African and Asian contexts, the bright appeal of the prosperity gospel even reaches into other religions. Therefore, it appears in many different forms and contexts (which is why we may also speak in the plural of prosperity gospels). Although the topos of wealth as an outward demonstration of divine grace is also controversial within

Pentecostal theology, it is almost synonymous with the Pentecostal movement, seeming at times to serve as a stereotype. The All African Conference of Churches (AACC) has dealt with the problem of prosperity theology in detail as part of its study process on "Discerning Misleading Theologies" in 2019.

Televangelism

Televangelism became known through the so-called "televangelists" and refers to the use of television as the preferred medium for spreading the Christian message of faith. The use of social mass media has its origins in the radio sermons of the 1920s and 1930s. Especially in the USA, independent radio and television stations were established under the names of leading preachers, churches and denominations, often associated with the Pentecostal movement and the charismatic renewal. Pioneers of televangelism such as Oral Roberts, Jim Bakker and Pat Robertson quickly made televangelism a Christian institution. The promise of supernatural signs and wonders, healings, exorcisms and prosperity, as well as reports of incidents of corruption, financial exploitation and double standards discredited television as a medium of Christian values. Nevertheless, the beginnings of televangelism must be seen as a missionary attempt to spread the gospel outside the churches. Proprietary broadcasting networks such as those of Pat Robertson (CBN) in the USA, Edir Macedo (RecordTV) in Brazil and the satellite broadcasting stations of Chris Oyakhilome in Nigeria, but also German TV stations such as Bibel TV, ERF and K-TV have largely detached televangelism from the person of the individual preacher. There are also clear attempts to use televangelism for social purposes. In an era of digital media that has moved away from traditional television, televangelism has also moved away from its original priority format of preaching. Today, it also serves to spread certain Christian messages and values among already converted believers.

Bibliography

Anderson, Allan Heaton, Spreading Fires. The Missionary Origins of Early Pentecostalism, Maryknoll, NY 2007.

Anderson, Allan Heaton, To the Ends of the Earth. Pentecostalism and the Transformation of World Christianity, Oxford 2013.

Anderson, Allan Heaton, An Introduction to Pentecostalism, Cambridge ²2014.

Andrée, Uta (Ed.), Einschätzungen zur Pfingstbewegung. Beiträge von Theologinnen und Theologen der Missionsakademie/Hamburg und der Faculdade Unida/Vitória (Theologische Impulse der Missionsakademie Bd. 12), Hamburg 2016.

Archer, Kenneth J., A Pentecostal Hermeneutic for the Twenty-First Century. Spirit, Scripture and Community, London 2004.

Bergunder, Michael/Haustein, Jörg (Eds.), Migration und Identität. Pfingstlich-charismatische Migrationsgemeinden in Deutschland, Frankfurt am Main 2006.

Brenner, Sven, Der angloamerikanische Einfluss auf die deutsche Pfingstbewegung, in: Frank Lüdke/Norbert Schmidt (Eds.), Die neue Welt und der neue Pietismus. Angloamerikanische Einflüsse auf den deutschen Neupietismus (Schriften der Evangelischen Hochschule Tabor 3), Berlin 2012.

Chitando, Ezra, Singing Culture. A Study of Gospel Music in Zimbabwe, Göteborg 2002.

Cunha, Magali do Nascimento, Fundamentalisms, the Crisis of Democracy and the Threat to Human Rights in South America: Trends and Challenges for Action. Engl. transl. by Samyra Lawall, Salvador (Bahia) 2020.

Dempster, Murray W./Klaus, Byron D./Petersen, Douglas (Eds.), The Globalization of Pentecostalism. A Religion Made to Travel, Carlisle 1999.

Evangelisches Missionswerk in Deutschland (Ed.), Studienheft: Heilung in Mission und Ökumene. Impulse zum interkulturellen Dialog über Heilung und kirchliche Praxis (Weltmission heute 41), Hamburg 2001.

Evangelische Zentralstelle für Weltanschauungsfragen, Die charismatische Bewegung in der DDR (EZW-Orientierungen und Berichte Nr. 10), Stuttgart 1980.

Fee, Gordon D., Wege zu einer paulinische Theologie der Glossolalie, in: *Haustein/Maltese* 2014 (s.u.), 93–106.

Freeman, Dena (Ed.), Pentecostalism and Development. Churches, NGOs and Social Change in Africa, Jerusalem 2012.

Gooren, Henri, Conversion Narratives, in: Allan Anderson/Michael Bergunder/André Droogers/Cornelis van der Laan (Eds.), Studying Global Pentecostalism. Theories and Methods, Berkeley/Los Angeles/London 2010, 93–112.

Haustein, Jörg, Writing Religious History: The Historiography of Ethiopian Pentecostalism, Wiesbaden 2011.

Haustein, Jörg/Fantini, Emanuele (Eds.), Pentecostalism in Ethiopia. Themenheft der Zeitschrift PentecoStudies, Jg. 12, Nr. 2, 2013.

Haustein, Jörg/Maltese, Giovanni (Eds.), Handbuch pfingstliche und charismatische Theologie, Göttingen 2014.

Hempelmann, Reinhard, Pfingstbewegung (Evangelische Zentralstelle für Weltanschauungsfragen – Kompaktinfos), Berlin 2015.

Hempelmann, Reinhard, Gottes Geist im Übernatürlichen? Wunder im Kontext pfingstlich-charismatischer Bewegungen, in: Matthias Pöhlmann (Ed.), Sehnsucht nach Heil. Wunderglaube als Herausforderung (EZW-Texte 262), Berlin 2019, 5–16.

Heuser, Andreas (Ed.), Pastures of Plenty. Tracing Religio-Scapes of Prosperity Gospel in Africa and Beyond, Frankfurt am Main/New York 2015.

Heuser, Andreas, Prosperity Theology: Material Abundance and Praxis of Transformation, in: Wolfgang Vondey (Ed.), The Routledge Handbook of Pentecostal Theology, Abingdon/New York 2020, 410–420.

Hocken, Peter/Richie, Tony L./Stephenson, Christopher A. (Eds.), Pentecostal Theology and Ecumenical Theology. Interpretations and Intersections (Global Pentecostal and Charismatic Studies Vol. 34), Leiden/Boston 2019.

Hollenweger, Walter J., Charismatisch-pfingstliches Christentum. Herkunft – Situation – Ökumenische Chancen, Göttingen 1997.

Johnson, David/Van Vonderen, Jeff, Geistlicher Missbrauch. Die zerstörende Kraft der frommen Gewalt (German translation by E. Weyandt), Wiesbaden 1996.

Kick, Annette/Hemminger, Hansjörg, Unabhängige Gemeinden neben Kirchen und Freikirchen (EZW-Texte 265), Berlin 2020.

Koehrsen, Jens, Middle Class Pentecostalism in Argentina. Inappropriate Spirits, Leiden/Boston 2014.

Krämer, Klaus/Vellguth, Klaus (Eds.), Pentekostalismus. Pfingstkirchen als Herausforderung in der Ökumene (Theologie der Einen Welt 15), Freiburg/Basel/Wien 2019.

Kürschner-Pelkmann, Frank, Reinhard Bonnke's Theology – A Pentecostal Preacher and His Mission. A Critical Analysis (translated by Cynthia C. Lies), Nairobi 2004.

Lüdke, Frank, Die Trennung von Pfingstbewegung und Gemeinschaftsbewegung, www.eh-tabor.de/de/die-trennung-von-pfingstbewegung-und-gemeinschaftsbewegung (retrieved on 13.5.2020).

Luhrmann, Tanja, Metakinesis: How God Becomes Intimate in Contemporary U. S. Christianity, in: American Anthropologist 106, 3 (2010), 66–78.

Lutheran-Pentecostal Study Group, Lutherans and Pentecostals in Dialogue, 2010, www.strasbourginstitute.org/wp-content/uploads/2012/08/Lutherans-and-Pentecostals-in-Dialogue-Text-FINAL.pdf (retrieved on 5.8.2020).

Lutherischer Weltbund, Die Selbstverpflichtungen des Lutherischen Weltbundes auf dem ökumenischen Weg hin zur ekklesialen Gemeinschaft, Genf 2018, www.lutheranworld.org/sites/default/files/2018/documents/dtpw-ecumenical_commitments_2018_de.pdf (retrieved on 5.8.2020).

Macchia, Frank D., The Spirit and Life: A Further Response to Jürgen Moltmann, in: Journal of Pentecostal Theology 5 (1994), 21–127.

Macchia, Frank D., Justified in the Spirit: Creation, Redemption, and the Triune God, Grand Rapids, MI 2010.

Moltmann, Jürgen, Der Geist des Lebens. Eine ganzheitliche Pneumatologie, München 1991.

Moltmann, Jürgen/Kuschel, Karl-Josef (Eds.), Pentecostal Movements as an Ecumenical Challenge (Concilium 1996/3), London 1996.

Myung, Sung-Hoon/Hong, Young-Gi (Eds.), Charis and Charisma. David Yonggi Cho and the Growth of Yoido Full Gospel Church, Oxford 2003.

Oduro, Thomas, Independent Churches in Africa (AICs), in: Isabel Phiri/Dietrich Werner (Eds.), Anthology of African Christianity, Oxford 2016, 431–440.

Onyinah, Opoku, Pentecostal Exorcism. Witchcraft and Demonology in Ghana, Dorset 2012.

Päpstlicher Rat zur Förderung der Einheit der Christen, Final report of the Dialogue between the Secretariat for Promoting Christian Unity of the Roman Catholic Church and Leaders of some Pentecostal Churches and Participants in the Charismatic Movement within Protestant and Anglican Churches (1972–1976), www.christianunity.va/content/unitacristiani/it/dialoghi/sezioneoccidentale/pentecostali/dialogo/documenti-di-dialogo/1976-rapporto-finale-/testo-in-inglese.html (retrieved on 11.7.2020).

Pobee, John/Ositelu II, Gabriel, African Initiatives in Christianity: The Growth, the Gifts and Diversities of Indigenous African Churches – a Challenge to the Ecumenical Movement, Geneva 1998.

Pöhlmann, Matthias/Jahn, Christine (Eds.), Handbuch Weltanschauungen, religiöse Gemeinschaften, Freikirchen, Gütersloh 2015.

Robeck, Cecil M. Jr./Yong, Amos (Eds.), The Cambridge Companion to Pentecostalism, New York 2014.

Schröder, Bernd, Erfahrung mit der Erfahrung – Schlüsselbegriff erfahrungsbezogener Religionspädagogik, in: ZfTK 95, 2 (1998), 277–294.

Steiner, Leonhard, Mit folgenden Zeichen. Eine Darstellung der Pfingstbewegung, Basel 1954.

Suarsana, Yan, Pandita Ramabai und die Erfindung der Pfingstbewegung. Postkoloniale Religionsgeschichtsschreibung am Beispiel des „Mukti Revival", Wiesbaden 2013.

Tempelmann, Inge, Geistlicher Missbrauch. Auswege aus frommer Gewalt. Ein Handbuch für Betroffene und Berater, Holzgerlingen [2]2018.

Vetter, Ekkehart, Jahrhundertbilanz – erweckungsfasziniert und durststreckenerprobt. Ein Beitrag zur Erweckungsgeschichte im 20. Jahrhundert und zur Entstehung der Pfingstbewegung in Deutschland. 100 Jahre Mülheimer Verband Freikirchlich-Evangelischer Gemeinden, Bremen 2009.

Vondey, Wolfgang (Ed.), Pentecostalism and Christian Unity: Ecumenical Documents and Critical Assessments, Eugene, OR 2010.

Vondey, Wolfgang (Ed.), Pentecostalism and Christian Unity. Vol 2: Continuing and Building Relationships, Eugene, OR 2013.

Vondey, Wolfgang, Die Theologie der Pfingstbewegung. Beiträge und Herausforderungen an die christliche Dogmatik, in: NZSTh 59 (2017), 427–446.

Welker, Michael, Gottes Geist. Theologie des Heiligen Geistes, Neukirchen-Vluyn 1992.

Welker, Michael (Ed.), The Work of the Spirit: Pneumatology and Pentecostalism, Grand Rapids, MI 2006.

Yong, Amos, Spirit – World – Community. Theological Hermeneutics in Trinitarian Perspective, Aldershot 2002.

Yong, Amos, Renewing Christian Theology. Systematics for a Global Christianity, Waco, TX 2014.

Zimmerling, Peter, Charismatische Bewegungen (UTB 3199), Göttingen ²2018.

Zimmerling, Peter, Die charismatischen Bewegungen. Theologie – Spiritualität – Anstöße zum Gespräch, Göttingen ²2002.

EKD Advisory Commission for Worldwide Ecumenism and further contributors

EKD Advisory Commission for Worldwide Ecumenism

- Director Christoph Anders, Hamburg (until 2019)
- Oberkirchenrätin Dr. Uta Andrée, Kiel (from 2019)
- Rev. Heike Bosien, Stuttgart
- Rev. Anne Freudenberg, Hamburg
- Rev. Dr. Dagmar Heller, Bensheim (from 2019)
- Prof. Dr. Claudia Jahnel, Bochum
- Rev. Jan Janssen, Rotterdam
- Rev. Kevin Jessa, Fürstenwalde
- Director Rainer Kiefer, Hamburg (Deputy Chair)
- Director Dr. Mareile Lasogga, Bensheim (until 2019)
- Prof. Dr. Ulrike Link-Wieczorek, Oldenburg (Chair)
- Rev. Britta Mann, Tübingen
- Oberkirchenrat Michael Martin, Munich
- Superintendent Philipp Meyer, Hameln
- Prof. Dr. Andreas Nehring, Erlangen
- Prof. Dr. Friederike Nüssel, Heidelberg
- Rev. Dr. Claudia Rammelt, Bochum
- Prof. Dr. Wilhelm Richebächer, Hermannsburg
- Rev. Dr. Martin Robra, Geneva (until 2019)
- Rev. Dr. Annegreth Schilling, Frankfurt
- Prof. Dr. Simone Sinn, Bossey (from 2019)
- Prof. Dr. Henning Theißen, Lüneburg
- Rev. Paula Trzebiatowski, Augsburg
- Oberkirchenrätin Marianne Wagner, Speyer (bis 2019)

Permanent guests of the Commission

- Bishop Petra Bosse-Huber, Hanover
- Bishop Dr. Michael Bünker, Vienna (until 2018)
- Director Prof. Dr. h. c. Cornelia Füllkrug-Weitzel, Berlin
- Dr. Stefan Jäger, Wuppertal
- Prof. Dr. Claudia Warning, Berlin (until 2018)
- Prof. Dr. Dietrich Werner, Berlin (from 2018)

Secretary

- Oberkirchenrat Prof. Dr. Martin Illert, Hanover (until 2019)
- Oberkirchenrat Dr. Olaf Waßmuth, Hanover (from 2019)

Working group "Pentecostal movement"

- Oberkirchenrätin Dr. Uta Andrée, Kiel
- Rev. Heike Bosien, Stuttgart
- Prof. Dr. Andreas Heuser, Basel (permanent guest)
- Prof. Dr. Claudia Jahnel, Bochum (Chair)
- Prof. Dr. Ulrike Link-Wieczorek, Oldenburg
- Rev. Dr. Annegreth Schilling, Frankfurt
- Prof. Dr. Henning Theißen, Lüneburg
- Rev. Paula Trzebiatowski, Augsburg
- Oberkirchenrat Dr. Olaf Waßmuth, Hanover (Secretary)
- Prof. Dr. Dietrich Werner, Berlin

The EKD Advisory Commission for Worldwide Ecumenism would like to thank the following experts who have contributed to the development of this study document by drafting texts for individual sections and/or by giving advice:

- Prof. Dr. Emmanuel Kwesi Anim, Accra/Ghana
- National Secretary Damaris Auwärter, Urbach
- Prof. Dr. Claudete Beise Ulrich, Vitória/Brazil
- Präses Marc Brenner, Urbach
- Prof. Dr. Peter Bubmann, Erlangen
- Prof. Dr. Moritz Fischer, Hermannsburg
- Dr. Maren Freudenberg, Bochum
- PD Dr. Martin Fritz, Berlin
- Prof. Dr. Jörg Haustein, Cambridge
- Rev. Dr. Reinhard Hempelmann, Berlin
- Prof. Dr. Sarah Hinlicky Wilson, Tokyo
- Prof. Dr. Werner Kahl, Hamburg
- Rev. Annette Kick, Stuttgart
- Prof. Dr. Miranda Klaver, Amsterdam
- Prof. Dr. Jens Köhrsen, Basel
- Prof. Dr. Andreas Krebs, Bonn
- Rev. Mike K. Lee, Düsseldorf
- Rev. Leita Ngoy, Dar es Salaam/Tanzania
- Rev. Dr. Gotthard Oblau, Essen
- Rev. Dr. Bernhard Olpen, Düsseldorf
- Dr. Jean-Daniel Plüss, Vitznau
- Kirchenrat Dr. Matthias Pöhlmann, Munich
- Prof. Dr. Cecil M. Robeck, Jr., Pasadena, CA/USA
- Rev. Dr. Liu Ruomin, Hamburg
- Dr. Paul Schmidgall, Freudenstadt
- Rev. Dr. Dirk Spornhauer, Bad Berleburg
- Prof. Dr. Yan Suarsana, Bremen

- Bischop Dr. Jack Urame, Lae/Papua New Guinea
- Prof. Dr. Wolfgang Vondey, Birmingham
- Lukas Werthschulte, Bochum